Weaving
Science Inquiry
and
Continuous
Assessment

Using Formative Assessment to Improve Learning

Maura O'Brien Carlson   Gregg E. Humphrey   Karen S. Reinhardt

Foreword by Susan Mundry

CORWIN PRESS, INC.
A Sage Publications Company
Thousand Oaks, California

For information:

Corwin Press, Inc.
A Sage Publications Company
2455 Teller Road
Thousand Oaks, California 91320
www.corwinpress.com

Sage Publications Ltd.
6 Bonhill Street
London EC2A 4PU
United Kingdom

Sage Publications India Pvt. Ltd.
B-42 Panchsheel Enclave
Post Box 4109
New Delhi 110 017 India

Printed in the United States of America

Library of Congress Cataloging-in-Publication Data

Carlson, Maura O'Brien.
Weaving science inquiry and continuous assessment : using formative assessment to improve learning / by Maura O'Brien Carlson, Gregg E. Humphrey, and Karen S. Reinhardt.
     p. cm.
Includes bibliographical and (p.   ) an index.
ISBN 0-7619-4589-X (Cloth) — ISBN 0-7619-4590-3 (Paper)
   1. Science—Study and teaching (Elementary) 2. Students—Rating of.
I. Humphrey, Gregg E. II. Reinhardt, Karen. III. Title.
LB1585.C29 2003
372.3'5044—dc211

2003004594

This book is printed on acid-free paper.

03   04   05   06   07   7   6   5   4   3   2   1

Illustrator: Jean Carlson Masseau, Hinesburg, VT

Acquisitions Editor:	Rachel Livsey
Editorial Assistant:	Phyllis Cappello
Production Editor:	Julia Parnell
Copy Editor:	Kristin Bergstad
Typesetter:	C&M Digitals (P) Ltd.
Proofreader:	Kathleen Pearsall
Indexer:	Pamela Van Huss
Cover Designer:	Michael Dubowe
Production Artist:	Lisa Miller

Contents

Foreword

Susan Mundry

Assessment of student learning has never been more important. State and local tests are being increasingly used to document levels of learning and build accountability into the education system. But educators committed to learning for all need more than standardized tests and end assessments. To meet the challenge of learning for all, teachers need processes and tools for monitoring student growth every day and over time.

The idea of using continuous classroom assessment every day to enhance teaching and learning evolved out of the authors' work with teachers to improve science education over many years. Beginning in the early 1990s, they worked with more than 250 teachers to improve science teaching and learning. They engaged teachers in learning science content through inquiry themselves, and created the environment and conditions for exploration. They focused on science topics in depth, and emphasized habits of mind associated with science—inquiry, skepticism, discovery, and collaboration. At the time, "science as inquiry" was a foreign concept to most teachers, and the *National Science Education Standards* (NRC, 1996) and *Benchmarks for Science Literacy* (AAAS, 1993) were still in development.

As the authors provided professional development in science they learned quite a bit about what teachers needed to use inquiry effectively. The open-ended nature of teaching science as inquiry thrust teachers into unknown territory. Along with their participating teachers, they began to raise questions about their role as the teacher and to ask, "What does it really look like to use inquiry in the classroom?" "How does one do it well?" and "When I use an inquiry approach, how do I know what students are learning? How do I assess student learning?"

Over time they realized effective teaching involved guiding students as they engaged in the inquiry process to ensure that students were productive and developed understanding of science concepts. They realized being a good facilitator of learning required knowing how children think about science concepts, recognizing misconceptions they often hold, and having strategies for challenging such misconceptions. To address this need, the authors began to weave instruction in science inquiry together with the practice of assessment.

This launched a new development in the work of the authors. Teachers learned to observe and listen closely to students in order to capture their ideas and abilities in the moment. With the teachers as co-developers, they created methods for day-to-day observation and documentation of students' work, thinking, and ideas. They worked closely with these teachers as they reflected on their classroom practices and were able to identify the strategies and the tools they found helpful. For example, the teachers became attuned to really listening to and gaining understanding of their students' scientific ideas. The authors worked with the teachers to help them with questioning techniques and introduced them to the strategy of having science conversations and "scientists' meetings" to learn what their students were thinking and able to do. Note taking, video- and audio taping, photographs, digital pictures, student writing, and student products took on a whole new meaning as they became simple "tools" of assessment. Many teachers told of ways they were now able to incorporate the data gained from using these tools as they applied them in their own classrooms.

The authors observed how using these techniques and tools in the classroom opened up a new world to teachers. Knowing how students were thinking about the science and what they were struggling with gave the teachers insight into how best to support learning. In real time, they saw how children truly "build" their understanding. The techniques and tools gave them the ability to see children's building blocks of understanding and help students modify those to reach higher understanding.

The idea of continuous assessment is simple, yet powerful. When teachers focus on students' ideas, they are able to make better decisions about instruction. They can become more deliberate about the hundreds of interactions they have with students every day. They can identify the concepts students are having trouble with and address them long before the state and local assessments are given and the results tabulated. In the case of the teachers involved in the project, using continuous or formative assessment increased their efficacy and their students' understanding of science and inquiry.

Continuous assessment as a way of monitoring student learning and helping teachers make better instructional choices is a valuable practice. Adding to its value is its contribution to teacher growth. As someone who designs and studies professional development programs, I see continuous assessment as a powerful mechanism for teachers to learn from their own practice. Examining student work and ideas has become recognized as a key strategy for teacher learning. As Loucks-Horsley, Hewson, Love, and Stiles (1998) write, "More learning occurs when teachers confront real problems—ones that they face in their classrooms on a daily basis. Such is the case with student work and assessments, which teachers use to judge the quality of learning and, in some cases, teaching" (p. 121).

The authors provide a rationale and practical tools for weaving continuous assessment and reflective instruction into the fabric of learning. Teachers who use the methods in the book will know what and how students are learning every day and will gain insights into how best to facilitate learning in their classrooms. Professional developers who model these practices now have a new resource for helping teachers to promote continuous classroom assessment.

—Susan Mundry

Preface

PURPOSE OF THE BOOK

If you are going to teach in an inquiry-based, content-rich way, how will you think about and facilitate assessment? This book is intended to provide you with the opportunity to examine your beliefs about the purposes of your own classroom assessment strategies and to contemplate the idea of formative assessment and how it fits into the larger view of other types of assessment. We hope you will consider how what we call "continuous" assessment can improve your interactions with your students and help you reflect on your own practices.

Our hope is that the descriptions, stories, strategies, and tools featured in this book will spark your interest and encourage you to examine your assumptions about teaching, learning, and assessment, and how these beliefs affect your students. Rather than prescribe recipes for success, the contents of this book are meant to stimulate your thinking. We hope they will inspire you to adapt the suggestions for facilitating science inquiry through continuous assessment to your own unique circumstances. We hope that by doing so you will experience the delight and growth in understanding that comes from listening to and engaging deeply with students. We hope that your efforts will catalyze meaningful changes in your students' thinking and learning. We also predict that once you employ these strategies in science, you will be prompted to use them to enhance teaching and learning in other disciplines.

RESEARCH BASE FOR THE BOOK

This book represents the authors' twelve years of intensive experience helping teachers integrate ongoing formative assessment with an inquiry approach to science. Funded by the National Science Foundation, our work is grounded in research about effective science teaching and learning conducted by the National Center for Improving Science Education, the National Research Council, and other science education reform initiatives. Specifically, we draw on the vision provided by the National Science Education Standards, which call for dramatic changes in instruction, assessment, and professional development, and that describe a way of science teaching and learning that reflects how science itself is done. That is, using an inquiry approach builds an understanding of the natural world; reflecting on both the inquiry process and the new understandings helps both the student and you, yourself, to grow.

Specifically, this book highlights learnings from the Continuous Assessment in Science Project (CASP) from 1995 to 1997, and a professional development materials grant: Strengthening Science Inquiry, Assessment and Teaching, from 1998 through 2002, both funded by the National Science Foundation. The CASP grant grew out of our belief that traditional end assessments do not accurately reflect the richness of the inquiry process, the growth in students' conceptual understandings, and the use of scientific processes and dispositions that occur throughout the learning process. Thus, the grant focused on helping teachers develop methods for assessing students' growth while facilitating science inquiry in the elementary and middle grades.

The methodology for this research included the efforts of forty-one teachers from thirteen schools as they participated in CASP. Together they helped us research and develop methods for assessing student learning that (a) were aligned with inquiry teaching and learning, (b) would accurately and completely represent students' growth in the concepts, processes, and dispositions of science, and (c) would allow for student engagement in the assessment process. These teachers collected data on how and what students were learning as they engaged in inquiry-based science in their classrooms. In a classroom research style, teachers determined questions about science teaching and learning that intrigued them, gathered data, and wrote about their observations and findings. Participants developed and tested a range of strategies and tools to facilitate student inquiry and document student progress. They also learned to analyze and use the data they gathered to monitor student growth, to adjust instruction to better meet students' developmental needs, to take student learning deeper, and to reflect on and improve their own practice.

This book presents a synthesis of the specific learnings of this project within the broader context of the authors' work in science education reform.

AUDIENCE FOR THE BOOK

This book is written primarily to the practicing teacher. It builds on what you already do—make decisions about instruction as you observe and listen to students—and suggests how to use this approach more deliberately to improve science teaching and learning in your classroom. Stories and suggestions from other fellow teachers in a range of classroom contexts reveal how you can use techniques such as "scientists' meetings" to facilitate science inquiry and conversations. They suggest how you can listen carefully and document student understanding and skills, then use the information gathered to deepen student learning. The stories featured in this book also reveal how striving to better understand, document, and guide students' thinking and learning will enhance your professional growth. Finally, the book will help you explore how to plan for the kind of professional development that can help you incorporate new approaches for facilitating and assessing inquiry-based teaching and learning.

If you are a professional development provider or administrator, the book can help you in your practices with teachers to integrate continuous assessment with science education and to use the resulting data to report students' progress. We hope that it will also help parents, community members, and policymakers to recognize the value of gathering and using this authentic classroom data at the local level for monitoring student growth, improving instruction, and helping teachers grow professionally.

BOOK ORGANIZATION

In writing this book about inquiry and continuous assessment, we quickly realized that while there are many good resources to help you understand inquiry, there is much less information about the type of formative assessment called for by the nature of inquiry itself. Therefore, in this book, we make the assumption that readers have a basic understanding of inquiry, and we concentrate our efforts on having the readers understand the essence of continuous assessment in the context of inquiry, and the strategies and tools for collection, analysis, and use of continuous assessment data.

The quotations from teachers, teacher educators, and program staff work to enhance the descriptions and understanding of this type of formative assessment. Vignettes of teachers and students practicing inquiry and continuous assessment are included to give pictures of what it can look like in the classroom setting.

The resources we used in writing the book along with other resources we feel would be helpful to further your knowledge base on the themes discussed in the chapters are listed at the end of the book.

Chapter 1 describes the uniqueness of continuous assessment as a teaching and learning strategy as well as a strategy integral to your own professional development. You will read about the importance of using this type of formative assessment for the benefit of your students, and as information to share with parents and other stakeholders. You will see how it matches your goals for student learning, and how it also serves many other purposes, including your own reflection on and self-improvement in your teaching. A picture of how this type of assessment fits into the larger view of assessment is captured in graphic form, and the techniques and tools of continuous assessment are introduced.

The chapter closes with a vignette of one teacher's classroom research around the questions he had about student conceptual development and his use of continuous assessment strategies and tools to help him find the answers he needed.

Chapter 2 anchors this type of assessment firmly in the context of inquiry-based learning. The chapter begins with a discussion of how trust in students and respect for their ideas form the underpinnings of inquiry learning and continuous assessment. A review of inquiry is given in writing and graphics, and the chapter continues with the idea of using continuous assessment within the context of inquiry. The vignette at the end gives a view of how both facilitating learning and continuously assessing become intertwined and at times indistinguishable from one another.

Chapter 3 provides more detail of each of the strategies and tools that can be used for facilitating and documenting the learning taking place in your classroom. Contexts, key elements, and implementation suggestions are given for each technique. Explanation of each of the documentation tools is included in the text, followed by a discussion of the advantages, and challenges of each tool. Voices from the field lend examples of actual classroom experiences to the discussion of each strategy and tool.

Chapter 4 makes the important point that what you do with the documentation is as important as your abilities to facilitate and collect it. This chapter discusses how to analyze and use continuous assessment data and reinforces the idea that knowing what you're looking for is key to being able to determine what and how the students are doing. Whether you're analyzing data on the spot during a class or listening to a tape on the way home from work, having in mind clear indicators of the skills, concepts, and dispositions necessary for scientific literacy is key. With these indicators in mind, you are able to use data to make decisions on the spot or for the next day, to take learning deeper, to enhance your own teaching skills, and to save pieces of data for summative reporting. Examples of all of these uses are provided, and a vignette at the end tells the story of how one teacher uses ongoing/continuous assessment throughout a unit on light.

Chapter 5 addresses the realities of implementing inquiry and continuous assessment in your classroom. Handling time challenges of inquiry and continuous assessment, integrating them with traditional testing, acquiring more content knowledge, managing continuous assessment, helping students engage deeply in their learning, resources, and parent involvement are addressed.

Chapter 6 describes ways in which continuous assessment data help teachers see ways to improve their own teaching practices of implementing inquiry and continuous assessment. This reflection and improvement is a kind of ongoing professional development for the teacher by her- or himself and together with peers. Later in the chapter a model of professional development is described that features inquiry and continuous assessment.

The Resources at the end of the book contain easy-to-use charts of the techniques, tools, purposes, and uses of continuous assessment and National Science Education Standards summary charts for assessment, content, teaching, program, district, and professional development standards.

HOW TO USE THE BOOK

Teachers can read the chapters and consider their own beliefs and practices for facilitating and assessing inquiry in science and other disciplines. Teachers in study groups can read, discuss, and try out ideas and strategies proposed in the book, and debrief their experiences and findings with their peers. Professional Developers and Teacher Leaders will find the book useful for their own understanding of inquiry and this type of formative classroom assessment as well as use the book with teachers in their courses and other professional development initiatives.

ACKNOWLEDGMENTS

This book is the culmination of working for over a decade with elementary and middle school students, teachers, and administrators. In 1990 we created a network of schools and teachers dedicated to carrying out recommendations as published by the National Center for Improving Science Education. With inspiration and support from Susan Loucks-Horsley, Susan Mundry, Senta Raizen, and many others from The NETWORK, Inc., we were able to create The Vermont Elementary Science Project thanks to funding from the National Science Foundation. The years of providing professional development and sustained support in science education for teams of teachers and administrators led to The Continuous Assessment in Science Project, also funded by the National Science Foundation, in which we refined the strategies and engaged in inquiry around the ideas that are represented in this book.

Instrumental in all of these endeavors has been our Senior Advisor, Susan Mundry, and our Senior Scientist, Bob Prigo. Bob's talent and vision for the role of content in the science education change process have been invaluable. Susan's faith in our work; her knowledge of teaching and learning and of teacher development; and her help in organization, planning, and implementing our ideas has been inspiring. The educators who used continuous assessment as a driving force in their classrooms and in their own professional development remain key people to whom we are indebted. These include:

A special thank-you to Graham Clarke and Pat Fitzsimmons for allowing us to use them as "case studies," and to Mary Abele-Austin, Steve Bless, Grace Freeman, Sharyl Green, Cyndy Hall, JoAnn Harvey, Carol Hinsdale, Mary Ladabouche, Denise Larrabee, Susan Linskey, Kathy Renfrew, Kurt Sherman Carol Slesar, Lynn Talamini-Hervey, Ginny Yandow, Janice Brisco, Lisa Charpentier, Lauren Kogge, Linda Peake, JoAnne Smith, and the Charlotte Elementary School students, teachers, and administrators.

We sought guidance and support from many other professional development educators from around the country as we refined the process of shaping the ideas for this book. They include: Tim Whiteford, Page Keeley, Doris Ash, Edith Beatty, Becky Dyasi and Hubert Dyasi, Meredith Wade, Casey Murrow, Frank Watson, John Tapper, Mike Jabot, Susan Holmes, Christina Johnson, and Tre Burke.

We are also indebted to our friends at Learning Innovations/WestEd who have helped and supported us in numerous ways: Eve Pranis, Deanna Bailey, Cheryl LaFrance, Cybele Werts, Jan Phlegar, Dolly Fleming, and Jane Nesbitt.

Finally, we wish to thank our NSF program officer, Janice Earle, for her guidance and support.

Corwin Press gratefully acknowledges the contributions of the following reviewers:

Joan Commons
Academic Coordinator
UCSD Center for Research in Educational Equity,
Assessment, and Teaching Excellence (CREATE)
La Jolla, California

Douglas Llewellyn
Visiting Professor
St. John Fisher College
Rochester, New York

Joani Harr
Middle School Math Teacher
Seattle School District
Seattle, Washington

Nancy Kellogg
Professional Development Coordinator
Center for Learning and Teaching in the West
Boulder, Colorado

Kathy DiRanna
K-12 Alliance Statewide Director
WestEd
Santa Ana, California

Anne Grall Reichel
Director of Science
Lake Forest School District 67
Lincolnshire, Illinois

Robert E. Yager
Professor of Science Education
University of Iowa
Iowa City, Iowa

Joni Falk
Principal Investigator
TERC
Cambridge, Massachusetts

Katherine E. Stiles
Senior Research Associate
WestEd
Indianapolis, Indiana

Linda Samuels
CEO
The Science of Learning Center
Chestnut Hill, Massachusetts

About the Authors

Maura O'Brien Carlson works to empower teachers in their understanding and practice of inquiry-based teaching and learning, and formative assessment. "I have the greatest respect for teachers and their contributions to the lives of children," says Maura. "They are the professionals in their field. They know each of their students' strengths and weaknesses and use developmentally appropriate strategies to work with the age group they teach. What we can offer these teachers is an opportunity to expand their view of teaching, assessment, and learning to include inquiry and continuous assessment."

Maura is Co-Director of the Center for Science Education and Professional Development, at Learning Innovations at WestEd. "In our professional development initiatives, we model good teaching and assessment practices for teachers and teacher educators," Maura explains. Recently, Maura, along with Karen Reinhardt and Gregg Humphrey, has been working on an NSF-funded project to develop materials for these teachers and professional developers that are user-friendly and portray what good science teaching, learning, and assessment look like. "Building expertise in your field means being deliberately reflective about your work with learners," Maura says. Teachers are better prepared to facilitate their students' learning when they are given opportunities to pursue their own inquiries in science and about science teaching and assessment. When teachers have occasions to reflect on their own practice and share with their peers, they are better able to catalyze and support their students' learning.

Prior to working on these projects Maura served as a research associate for the National Center for Improving Science Education and co-authored two of the Center's major reports, and the book, *Elementary School Science for the '90s.* She has co-directed three large NSF-funded grants from 1990 to the present. Maura, along with other leaders in Vermont, has been instrumental in the development of a vision for systemic change in the State for science education. In this capacity she has served as one of the Co-Principal Investigators, and as a Professional Development Specialist, for the Vermont Statewide Systemic Initiative. In her evaluation work, she has been a part of evaluation teams for three NSF-funded initiatives. Her background includes teaching elementary science methods courses at the University of Vermont and twelve years teaching science at the middle and secondary school levels. She holds a Bachelor's of Science degree in Biology from Trinity College, and a Master's in Education and Environmental Studies from the University of Vermont, both located in Burlington, Vermont.

Maura is an outdoor enthusiast and enjoys hiking and cross-country skiing. In the summer you can find her in her perennial garden.

Gregg E. Humphrey believes you teach the way you are taught. With this in mind, Gregg's courses are inquiry-based, with students taking an active role as preservice teachers. As the Director of Elementary Teacher Education at Middlebury College, he works directly with the Middlebury community. Each preservice student is assigned to a classroom in an elementary school within the Addison Central Supervisory Union where they apply the ideas emerging from their course work.

Gregg is very familiar with the schools and teachers of Addison County due to his work of over thirty years in this area. He is a graduate of Middlebury College (1970) and spent eighteen years at Mary Hogan Elementary School in Middlebury. He was a classroom teacher, assistant principal, science curriculum coordinator, and Title I director during his time at Mary Hogan and Addison Central Supervisory Union. Along with Bob Prigo, Middlebury College physicist, Maura O'Brien Carlson of Learning Innovations at WestEd, and colleagues from around Vermont and the Northeast, Gregg co-directed three large National Science Foundation grants aimed at reforming elementary science. In this capacity he worked with teams of teachers, teacher leaders, and administrators locally, regionally, and nationally to support an inquiry approach to science and the professional development needed to sustain teaching improvement. He has produced a series of videotapes, and has authored articles on science inquiry-based teaching and learning, continuous assessment, and change initiatives in science education. His current research is in the area of formative assessment as a driving force behind both student and teacher development.

Gregg holds a Bachelor's in Sociology and Anthropology from Middlebury College, Middlebury, Vermont, and a Master's in Administration and Planning with emphasis on curriculum and instruction, from the University of Vermont, Burlington. He has a passion for golf, bluegrass music (his music group is known as Snake Mountain Bluegrass), and cooking!

Karen S. Reinhardt is a former Co-Director of the Center for Science Education after working at the Center as a Program Associate for several years prior to becoming Co-Director.

Karen's responsibilities at the Center included working with the project team on a National Science Foundation–funded grant to develop video and print materials for professional developers helping teachers incorporate inquiry-oriented science and continuous assessment into their classrooms. She also provided direct professional development services in science inquiry and continuous assessment to teachers, teacher leaders, and other professional developers, both locally and nationally.

Prior to working at the Center, Karen served as Professional Development Coordinator for the National Gardening Association in Burlington, Vermont. While there she directed the professional development component of the National Science Foundation–funded Growing Science Inquiry Project. This role included working with leadership teams of teachers, administrators, and horticultural partners in twelve school districts nationally to support teachers to implement inquiry-based science with plants. As part of this work, she co-authored the Growlab Consultants' Toolkit and the Windows on the Classroom video series and Facilitator's Guide.

Karen has a Bachelor's degree in Child Study from Tufts University, and was the recipient of the Eliot Pearson Department of Child Study Award for outstanding scholarship and teaching potential. She holds a Vermont Level II: Professional Educator's License, with endorsements in Early Childhood and K-6 Education. Karen began graduate study in educational administration in July 2002.

The Essence of Continuous Assessment

1

WHAT IS CONTINUOUS ASSESSMENT?

"Continuous Assessment is listening closely to students, observing students as they are engaged in learning, as they are engaged with materials, and trying to understand what they understand."

—Program Associate

Every day, you, as teachers everywhere do, observe your students, listen to their conversations, and talk with them about their ideas, writings, and drawings. Always striving to understand and expand students' thinking and skills, you use the daily input you gather to decide what next steps you'll take to support their growth. When these things are done in a purposeful way, they become a kind of formative assessment we refer to as "continuous" assessment or "everyday" assessment.

"The best way I can describe continuous assessment is the process of learning to be with children in such a way as to understand their thinking so that you can continually expand, challenge, and scaffold each child's experiences."

—Kindergarten Teacher

We choose the phrase "continuous assessment" to describe a type of assessment that happens in real time rather than at the end of a week or unit. It is continuous/ongoing because it involves daily observations and documentation of students' work while they are engaged in inquiry investigations and discussions. This is not to say you are conducting assessments all of the time, but rather, you weave assessment strategies in with your facilitation techniques. At times, your assessment is indistinguishable from your teaching.

> *"Teachers see that they don't have to wait until the unit is done and the test is given and graded to find out how their students are doing. They can gather the information right then and there while the students are exploring their ideas."*

> —Project Co-Director

In the Educational Testing Service (1995) document, *Capturing the Power Classroom Assessment*, this type of assessment is referred to as Naturalistic assessment: "Naturalistic assessment refers to evaluation that is rooted in the natural setting of the classroom and involves observation of student performance in an informal context." The description goes on to say that documentation is the method for this type of assessment. "Documentation, a naturalistic method, is a process of classroom observation and record keeping over time, across learning modalities, and in coordination with colleagues."

In the inquiry-based classroom, continuous assessment is crucial to student learning. Because students' understanding and skills unfold naturally as they work with materials and explore their ideas through investigations and discussions, it is important that you be present. Being there to interact with your students both as a facilitator and an assessor, you can gather important information while the students are engaged in inquiry. Keeping track of this information and analyzing the data can help you to understand your students' thinking, and to monitor their growth in the concepts, processes, and dispositions of science. When students become "stuck" and need guidance, your intervention can help them delve deeper and move forward in their understanding. You can be as inquiry-oriented as your students by observing, recording, analyzing, and using the data you collect as they do their work.

> Continuous assessment has a lot to do with how well inquiry-based science actually functions, not only in the classroom but also in the real scientific world. It's about how scientists actually go about doing good science—in a process-oriented and inquiry-oriented way.

> As a teacher, you guide students along a path to the content that you want them to master down the line. It is not something where you can just intervene here or there, and think they are going to end up at the right point, in terms of national standards or whatever. You've got to be there, listening to them, interacting with them when they are manipulating the equipment, and have a question about it or are starting to see

a pattern. That is the time for you to reinforce those ideas, especially if they are ideas that are important down the line for conceptual understanding. (Bob Prigo, in *The Essence of Continuous Assessment*, Center for Education and Professional Development, 2001)

CONTINUOUS ASSESSMENT IN THE "BIG PICTURE" OF ASSESSMENT

"One component of my teaching that I have developed through my work with continuous assessment is that I have started documenting what we are doing in my science classroom. The biggest 'aha' for me was that assessment isn't an end; it's a beginning, prompting further investigation by the kids. Assessment didn't turn out to be a culminating thing like I thought it was, but a starting point for more learning."

—Third-Grade Teacher

The more this teacher practiced using continuous assessment in her classroom, the more she realized that assessment isn't always an end activity. Many of us, because of our own education experience, have the conception of assessment as an end-of-the-week, or end-of-a-unit event. Many of us make assumptions when we hear the word *assessment*. We assume that assessment means there is an item or task to complete; that assessment(s) happen after the students have completed a strand or unit, or outside of the time devoted for instruction; that assessments are given to see if the student "got it"; that an assessment is often in the form of a product, artifact, or investigation that the teacher evaluates outside of classroom time; and that good assessment(s) often comes from an external source. Many of us think of assessment as traditional tests and quizzes. Students often think of assessment as

What do you think of when you hear the word *assessment*? At a recent conference, we began our presentation by asking the participants—teachers, administrators, professional development providers—if they would write a few words or phrases that come to mind when they hear the word assessment. Here are some samples: Assessment = Traditional Tests, . . . the culmination of the unit, . . . standardized, . . . formal, . . . unpopular, . . . students' perspective: good–bad, pass–fail, . . . pressure for kids to do well; and if you don't do well, there is no going back, . . . value judgment, . . . paper and pencil, . . . high stakes, . . . state proficiency, . . . standardized statewide tests, . . . confusion over the use of classroom assessment, . . . SAT, . . . report card, . . . grades. Once these ideas were out in the open and recognized as commonly held conceptions, we continued our session and offered our participants a chance to learn about and experience continuous assessment as an important strategy to practice while students are engaged in normal everyday work.

a practice conducted for the sole purpose of grading, yet the feedback they get from these assessments often identifies for them what they don't know, rather than what they do know. Often times the words *assessment* and *testing* are used synonymously, while the reality is that assessment has many different meanings depending on the context.

Continuous assessment is *formative* by nature. The key here is that the collection of data about students' understanding of concepts, and their practice of the processes and habits of mind of science happens while the students are engaged in learning. When these data are used by teachers to make decisions about next steps for a student or group of students, to plan instruction, and to improve their own practice, they help *inform* as well as *form* practice; this is *formative assessment.* When data are collected at certain planned intervals, and are used to show what students have achieved to date, they provide a *summary* of progress over time, and are *summative* assessment. Both types of assessment are important and useful for the purposes they serve. The greatest benefit to students is when there is alignment of what is valued in science learning across the continuum of formative to summative assessments. In the section in Chapter 5 titled, "Challenge: How Do I Integrate Continuous Assessment With Traditional Testing?" you will see a more detailed discussion of differences between and value of both formative and summative assessments.

To see what continuous assessment is and is not, and to recognize that different assessments have different purposes and result in different types of data, see the graphic in Figure 1.1. It describes the niche this type of assessment has in the continuum of assessment types.

In the top section of the graphic are three important things to consider when planning for assessment: the purpose of the assessment; who is using the information (the audience); and what is being assessed, or, as we like to say, what is valued in science learning. Being clear about whether you are seeking information about individuals or information about the program will help you to match the assessment type to the appropriate strategies.

The Purpose and Use of Your Assessment

The use of the information you gather about student learning is what is important here. Are you gathering information in order to provide documentation of individual students' progress over time? Is it a way to convey your expectations to students? Will the information be used to guide or change your instruction? If it is any one or all of these, then the focus of your assessment is formative and is on individual students. If, instead, the data are collected for the purpose of monitoring the outcomes of a body of students and are to be used to provide a basis for planning and implementing improvements to a program, or to provide guidance for the allocation of resources to the program, materials, or

Figure 1.1   The Big Picture of Assessment

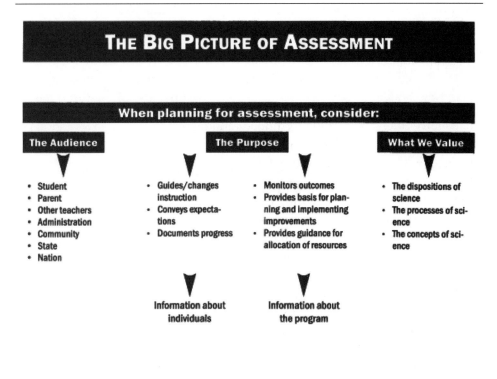

* Adapted from Focus 28, Capturing the Power of Classroom Assessment, Educational Testing Service, Princeton, NJ, 08541-0001. 1995.

the school building, then the assessment is most likely to be summative and to focus on the program.

What You Value (What You Want Students to Know and Be Able to Do)

Much research and attention to best practice has led to development of the *National Science Education Standards* (National Research Council, 1996; see more in Chapter 4). You will recognize these standards as the targets for student learning in science and therefore what ought to be taught and assessed:

- *The dispositions of science* (such as being able to use evidence to propose explanations, being willing to revise explanations as a result of new evidence or discussion, being open-minded, being able to persevere, etc.)
- *The processes of science* (such as identifying questions, observing systematically, measuring accurately, controlling variables, etc.)
- *The concepts of science* (such as, properties of matter, diversity and adaptations of organisms, the Earth in the solar system, etc.)

The Audience

If the audience is at the national or state level, the evaluation strategy will be summative and more formal than classroom assessment. Standardized tests and state portfolios are examples. If the audience is the students themselves, parents, or other teachers, then you will find it most helpful to use formative assessment strategies such as continuous assessment.

At the bottom of Figure 1.1 you will see a continuum of assessment strategies. Continuous assessment has its own unique position in the overarching concept of assessment. It does not take the place of, but rather provides completion to a continuum of assessment that starts in the classroom and culminates in formal program assessments. Continuous assessment is placed at the far left end of the continuum as formative assessment. What this kind of assessment looks like and how its data can be used is the subject of the remainder of this book. Placed on the far right of the continuum are examples of summative assessment, including formal program assessments like standardized tests. In between these endpoints we see some strategies such as portfolios and performance tasks—types of assessment that have both formative and summative characteristics.

Challenges may arise when one or another of the elements in the big picture is not considered; or when an assessment is used in a way for which it wasn't intended, such as choosing an assessment that can't provide the information needed or using the information in a way that doesn't match the purpose, the audience, or what is valued. For example:

- *Purpose:* A school district may send students' standardized test information to parents as a courtesy. Even if district administrators state that the results are used only to inform programmatic decisions, parents often interpret these results as the definitive say on their individual child's progress in the subject areas tested. Having received these results from the school district, parents may also assume that other assessments, such as classroom assessments, are less important than the standardized test.

• *What is valued:* A teacher may do an assessment but may not be clear about what she is looking for, that is, what she values as "good" science learning. In this case, she may pay attention to only the most easily observed information, such as how well students work together, whether they know facts, and whether or not their science notebooks are neat. In contrast, if she were clear about the processes and dispositions of science she wanted students to practice and the concept(s) she wanted them to develop, she could focus on these in her assessment and gather information about student progress that would be much more useful to both her and her students.

• *Use:* When a district places a heavy emphasis on test scores to evaluate teachers, they send a message that the standardized test score is what really counts. Standardized test scores are not meant to evaluate individual teachers, but to inform program decisions. Teacher evaluation should take place within the school setting and between the school or district administrator and the teacher. Another result of the use of these test scores to evaluate teachers is that teachers may start to put less emphasis on their own classroom data and begin to teach to the test.

Quite a bit has been written about formal or summative assessment. The focus of this book will be on continuous assessment—the day-to-day observation/documentation of normal work for the purpose of moving students forward in their understanding and practice of science.

TECHNIQUES AND TOOLS FOR CONTINUOUS ASSESSMENT

The techniques of continuous assessment listed below will not necessarily be new to you. In fact, you will recognize these techniques not only as good assessment strategies, but as excellent teaching strategies as well. These, when combined with some familiar tools, help you to gain and document information about students' understanding of science concepts, the practice of scientific dispositions, and the development of the processes of science (see Resource A for user-friendly charts that summarize the techniques and tools of continuous assessment).

Techniques for Continuous Assessment

- *Sitting and Listening Closely*. Teachers watch the behavior of the students at work and listen closely to their conversations. At times, they may ask questions during conversations to clarify details about what students are doing and what they are finding out, but otherwise do not interfere.
- *Purposeful Questioning*. Teachers ask open-ended questions that enable students to reflect on, clarify, and explain their thinking and actions and give their point of view during investigations.
- *Sharing New Material/Information*. Teachers give students new materials or information to help them move deeper in their inquiry.
- *Sparking Science Conversations*. Teachers structure opportunities for whole-class, group, and individual conversations to explore the learning occurring through the inquiry.
- *Student Self-Assessment*. Students conduct routine reflection.

Tools for Continuous Assessment

- Teacher's observation notes
- Videotape
- Audiotape
- Photographs
- Student science writing
- Artifacts and products of student science

You will see a more thorough description of the benefits of each technique and tool, and an explanation of how each can be used to enhance student learning, in Chapter 3, "Techniques and Tools for Facilitating Inquiry and Collecting Student Data."

WHY USE CONTINUOUS ASSESSMENT?

Black and Wiliam (1998) use the metaphor of the classroom as a "black box" to describe what the public, school administrators, and the media often focus on regarding assessment. In this model, inputs (e.g., curriculum requirements) go into the black box and outputs (e.g., test results) come out. There is often little attention paid to whether the students actually understand the concepts, but rather whether they can pass the tests. In contrast, continuous assessment uses the black box of the classroom as the site for an ongoing inquiry into what and how the students are learning. This collection of data, in conjunction with performance tasks and standardized tests, provides a more complete picture of what students have learned.

There are a number of benefits for you and your students when you start using continuous assessment in your classroom. The following is a sample of the benefits and reasons this type of assessment is so useful (a summary of these benefits is found in Resource A under "The Purposes and Uses of Continuous Assessment").

Serves Instruction While Monitoring Growth

By using continuous assessment strategies and tools, you are able to capture what your students are doing with and without your intervention. Whether you are a removed observer or sitting and listening closely as you watch your students and document what you see, the information you glean helps you to determine next steps to support their growth. At times this support is immediate and happens in the moment you suggest a new material for a group of students to use in their investigation, or help a student further understand a concept by offering an explanation.

Other times the information helps you decide what to do the next day. For instance, hearing a misconception like "all fruits float" helps you to think what you might do the next day. You may decide to bring in some different fruits to initiate an investigation to help the students see that while many fruits float, some sink, and to consider the factors of floating and sinking. This discussion may lead to other questions such as, "Do fruits that float, still float without their skins?" "What about vegetables? Do they sink or float?"

Consideration of how you might support your students' development over the long term is another benefit/use of the data you collect. You may also find yourself thinking about what you will do in next week's class or during next month's unit.

> Students in a fourth-grade class were given several liquids to explore. They tried various "tests" on these liquids. One group of three girls was working on an investigation to see what size and shape a drop of liquid would become when dropped on a piece of waxed paper. When the teacher stopped by to see what they were doing, she noticed that the girls were making a data table of the liquids, including the diameter of each drop. They were using such words as "small," "medium," and "large" when it came to recording the diameter or size of the "spread" of each of the drops. The teacher left the group for a minute and came back with rulers in her hand. She made the suggestion to the group to, "See what you can tell me about each of the drops by using this measuring instrument." In this case, the teacher seized the moment to teach these students about the importance of accuracy and the use of tools in scientific measurement.

Enhances Student Learning

You will find you are able to catalyze "deeper" thinking and understanding as students reflect on their own investigative processes and experiences. Reviewing a portion of a videotape of class discussion is one example. After watching a video clip of an initial scientist meeting at the beginning of a unit on motion, one student was able to describe a change in his conceptual understanding. He described what he originally thought would happen when his group rolled balls of various sizes and weights on linoleum and carpeted floors. Because the more massive balls rolled farther on the linoleum floor, he thought that the more massive balls would also roll farther on the rug. What he actually found out is that in some cases the less massive balls rolled farther than the more massive balls. After talking with the students in his group, other students, and the teacher, and continuing to experiment further, he determined that the rug provided a certain amount of interference for objects of different masses. He compared what he thought at the beginning of the unit to what he now understood about mass and friction, and the data he collected showing how the resistance of the rug affected the results of the trials on both surfaces. During the process, he was beginning to think that the angle of the "ramp" might also have something to do with his results.

Using continuous assessment data to provide timely feedback throughout an investigation encourages students to expand their thinking, modify their investigation, and revise their ideas while the investigation is still going on.

Continuous assessment also enhances student learning in an inquiry-based classroom when the students and teacher work together to articulate a vision of "good science." Just as the national committees did when developing the National Science Education Standards, when you work with your students in their science investigations, you can help them see that what they're doing is considered "good science." They begin to realize that when they make a careful observation, when they make a table to organize their data, when they communicate their findings to the group, they are doing the same things that scientists do. Pointing these things out helps students recognize what is valued so they can work toward concrete learning goals and identify their own growth. If you keep a list of these indicators posted, you'll find that in addition to it being a guide for you, the students can use the list to self-assess how they are doing in science. In Chapter 2, you will see a similar list that teachers in a professional development institute created for themselves to refer to "on the run."

Enables Teachers' Professional Growth

By striving to better understand and guide students' thinking and learning, you can become more reflective about your own practices and refine your teaching strategies. As a result of looking closely and sharing experiences with colleagues, you can develop new perspectives about how teaching, assessment, and learning interact and consider adjustments you might make in your teaching. One teacher reported,

> *"I was getting to each group and taking notes about each individual. But it didn't feel right. I felt rushed and not very effective. So I reflected and talked it over with my fellow teachers in my science study group and began to see what was happening. . . . I needed to stop being a walking report card data collector and get back to facilitating good science practices."*

—Fourth-Grade Teacher

As soon as this teacher became more of a researcher into what her students were thinking and doing and less of a collector of information for end evaluations such as report cards, she was able to reflect on her practice. She decided to focus on becoming a better listener.

Provides Information to Report Students' Progress

While the main purpose of using continuous assessment techniques is to inform decision making and professional practice, there is a strong summative component to this formative process. Over time the documentation of the evolution of students' understandings, skills, and science dispositions can be accumulated and can provide a wealth of data for reporting student progress and development for occasions such as report cards, science nights, and parent conferences.

As you read on in this book, you will see that we use the context of science inquiry to describe this type of formative assessment. Continuous assessment is not a specialized method designed for science alone. Rather, its methodology is useful for all areas of learning.

The *National Science Education Standards* (NRC, 1996), *Classroom Assessment*, and the *National Science Education Standards* (NRC, 2001), call for changes in the ways we assess. These NSES (National Science Education Standards) reports call for less emphasis on (but not the exclusion of) traditional views of assessment, and more emphasis on assessment of what is highly valued in learning: rich, well-structured knowledge, and understanding and reasoning. They also call for the involvement of students in their own assessment. See Resource B, Table B.1, "NSES: Changing Emphases for Assessment," for a summary of these Standards.

In the following chapters we discuss many aspects of continuous assessment: the context for continuous assessment, teaching beliefs that support it, the techniques and tools, and the analysis that promotes the use of the data. We will begin to address the challenges of facilitating inquiry and continuous assessment. And finally, we offer you a description of professional development that will help you use children's everyday experiences to inform instruction and your own teaching practices.

Vignette
Continuous Assessment

ONE TEACHER'S EXPERIENCE

Even though I was an experienced fifth- and sixth-grade teacher, teaching science was a challenge. I had little interest in science, and had avoided those courses throughout high school and college. This was especially true of the physical science content. I knew little of the content I was supposed to cover.

Learning to Facilitate Inquiry

One of the first units I was supposed to teach was a motion unit, complete with balls, ramps, and other materials. Throughout the unit, groups of students rotated through several stations, each with a card explaining how they should explore the materials. I only focused on making sure that the students saw the intended phenomena that each material could provide. When students used the materials in ways other than what was described by the task card, I was quick to correct them. I asked them not to explore other ideas or share their station results with others. I didn't want to spoil the surprise for groups who had not yet worked on a certain activity, presuming that only one surprise was possible—the one directed by the activity card.

When I visited one of my students at one of the motion stations, she asked, "What is supposed to happen with this stuff?"

"The card just asks that you observe what happens," I replied.

"Well, Mr. Clarke, it's supposed to do something that you want or else you wouldn't have us doing it."

At the end of the unit, I must admit that I found myself bored by my students' oral reports, which reflected the same structured approach that I had used in the investigation. Could this boredom have been a result of simply going through the motions of what I imagined was inquiry? If I was trying to get students to just verify science concepts, was that real inquiry? Was that real science? I wondered how to change the mechanical feel toward science that both my students and I experienced.

For a science unit later that year, I decided to use some assessment approaches (that I had learned in the Continuous Assessment in Science Project), which focused on student conceptual development. I began by brainstorming a list of questions about my science teaching and about my students:

What ideas do my students have about particular science concepts?

How do these change over time?

How can I begin to really listen to the ideas of my students?

How do student conceptions change as a result of focused inquiry investigations?

How can I stimulate more free-flowing discussions in science—ones that are more like the discussions we have when my students talk about characters in books or current events?

How can I stimulate both classroom science inquiry and student discussion?

How can I extend the initial stages of the inquiry process into fuller, more complete investigations?

I was interested both in conducting my own inquiry into my students' understanding of science concepts and in trying to refine my methods of science teaching. My plan was to use my list of questions as a guide.

I started by planning a "waves circus," a set of activity stations with hands-on materials and written questions that encourage exploration of these materials. As I unpacked the Slinkies, ropes, sheets, rubber hoses, and water troughs for the next day's opening lesson, I started jiggling things around to satisfy my own curiosity. As I shook a long silver spring attached to an eyehook I realized that I was doing my own inquiry, learning about waves! I noticed that I could generate different patterns depending on how quickly or slowly I shook the stretched spring. I watched the waves rebounding back at me when they reached the opposite wall. This was fun! Maybe, I thought, my students could learn about wave patterns and have fun too.

Recording and Reflecting on Continuous Assessment Data

I announced on the first day of the explorations: "Now that I've shown you all the materials and you know who your partners are, your directions for each of the stations will be the same. Use the materials to make waves and observe what happens. Discuss what you see and what you learn with your partners. I won't be interrupting you much. Instead, I'll be watching and listening and trying to write down what I hear you talking about." The students wriggled with anticipation.

Although my students worked in small groups and at workstations like they had in the motion study, there the similarities ended. Gone were my precise direction cards. Gone was the expectation that the students on this first day would record voluminous observations as they were working with the materials. Gone was my frenetic Groucho Marx–like classroom management, where I had darted from group to group asking clipped questions and hearing, but not truly listening to their ideas, all the while scanning the room for behaviors that weren't in sync with the direction cards. Small groups of students circulated from station to station reading the task cards, and interacting with Slinkies, jump ropes, water in long troughs, an oscilloscope (that I borrowed from a teacher at a nearby college), and with objects placed on a stretched bed sheet. As the student scientists went about their tasks, I listened closely to their comments, and made notes as I went along. I also used a tape recording to capture students discussing their investigations.

We even invented a way of talking about student investigations that we called "Tell and Show," which allowed students who hadn't been to a particular station to see what other students had learned there. Students insisted on both talking about and demonstrating what they had learned when they reported out to the class. By doing this we generated a class list of questions:

What is really moving in a wave?

How do waves begin?

What are different kinds of waves?

What are some differences and similarities of waves in various media?

Just what are waves and how do they move?

That night when I transcribed the notes onto the computer, I was amazed by the comments of one student, Josh. During the activity Josh had actually directed the group, advised on how to use the bed sheet, and had offered an idea about extending the activity. Here it was mid-February and the first time I'd heard Josh's "science voice" all year! It wasn't just that Josh spoke so much as it was the ease with which he participated and the confidence he displayed that caused me to reassess my view of his skills. Until that day I had witnessed a kid who was not interested much in school, displayed language limitations, and was unexcited about the possibilities of learning (or at least those that had, to date, been offered to him).

In the waves exploration, Josh's true voice had been heard sharing ideas about something in which he was clearly interested. I had a hunch that one reason he was so much more involved was because I wasn't speaking with or asking questions of the group. By remaining silent, I got out of my students' way and let the conversation develop among them and at their own level.

Over the next week, I transcribed some of the discussion comments from my notes and the audiotape. I made copies for the students, and they were very enthusiastic about seeing their spoken words in print. Even the slower readers devoured the transcriptions, scanning the text for their own names and their comments.

After a few mornings of the groups circulating through the wave stations, each group selected a station with which to begin a more extended inquiry investigation, articulating their own "investigable questions" and collecting data to test their ideas. One group was interested in finding a way to record the movement of a wave on paper. They decided to attach a Magic Marker to a Slinky in such a way that, as they generated various Slinky waves, the marker jiggled designs on some paper. I could hear their excitement as they honed their Slinky jiggling technique and discussed ways to improve the performance of their invention in order to get better and better "jiggle tracks," some of which I recorded with a video camera.

Sharing Continuous Assessment Data
With Students to Deepen Conceptual Understanding

One of the students asked if she could watch the video that we had been making, which had picked up the wave motion when one student moved the Slinky back and forth on the rug and when another student twisted the Slinky like a giant screw. As the students watched the tape, I encouraged them to look carefully at both the Slinky movement and the drawings, and they began to point out the different kinds of waves and the various ways that the marker moved. Afterwards, they wrote and drew diagrams in their "science jotters" explaining the various wave patterns. These jotters encourage many forms of keeping investigation notes: pictures with labels, lists, and charts, along with written comments. The data took on a life of their own as students became more and more engaged with thinking about what had happened. Their reflections caused us to ask, "What could be measured in a given wave? What words do scientists use to describe waves? How else could you generate a Slinky wave?"

Toward the end of the unit we had a science discussion group where I asked the class to look at the transcripts that I had made of their initial wave discussions. I asked, "Have any of your ideas changed?"

"Oh yes," said one girl, and pointed out a remark she had originally made. "Remember what I thought then? It's on page two; the part about waves bouncing off each other? Well, now I think they pass through each other because of the experiment we did today." The discussion was animated, and the students often used examples from their investigations to show what they had learned.

Reflecting on Continuous Assessment
Data to Inform Teacher Practice

Reflecting on what had occurred over the few weeks of this investigation was an exciting and humbling experience. Exciting, because I vaguely sensed being on the verge of possibilities—for myself as a teacher, and for the students and me as learners. It was humbling, and oddly unnerving, because I wasn't involved in the students' learning experiences in any of the ways that I had been throughout my previous teaching experience. I remembered that my visceral reaction of excitement was tempered by my discomfort in having been actively "invisible" at times in the classroom that first morning. My own understanding of the role of a teacher in a science-learning environment was in a state of disequilibrium.

My science teaching is now layered with daily discussions among my students and me, and among the students themselves, and with self-reflective moments in their writings and drawings that lead to new questions, further investigations, and conceptual growth. I have begun to witness students taking risks and shedding old ideas, and replacing them with newer, more sophisticated understandings that are based on real-life experiences.

My classroom has become one that honors reflection, revisiting, and documenting. I have begun to open up my students to their own ideas, as well as to the concepts, processes, and dispositions of science. I had explored student knowledge that I never knew existed, and learned more effective ways to facilitate an inquiry approach. As a result of my success in this new approach, assessment has become a driving force behind my teaching rather than an end product.

I continue to tinker with and improve my strategies, and have found that the habit of science discussion has become well established. This habit was evident in a recent language arts class when we were preparing to begin a biography of Benjamin Franklin. When I got to the part about "preparing a question about the book that could lead to a good discussion with your classmates," my student Eliza asked: "Like we do for science discussion groups?"

"Yes," I replied with a chuckle, "Like we do for science groups."

—Graham Clarke,
Sixth-Grade Teacher

The Context for Continuous Assessment

2

Student Inquiry

Students engage in investigations of their questions about the natural world in much the same way scientists do. They explore their ideas through hands-on experiences, analyzing and interpreting the information they collect along the way. At each step, they communicate findings and discuss their ideas with others. In synthesizing their ideas to create explanations, they connect what they already know about the phenomena with the new knowledge gained from their investigations, your explanations, and other scientific resources. Throughout the process other questions emerge, and the inquiry cycle begins again.

Continuous assessment, likewise, is an inquiry into student learning. You can consider the questions you have about students' growth and collect formative data about conceptual understanding and demonstration of science processes and dispositions *at every phase of investigation*. You will find you can analyze these data in the moment and over time in order to make judgments about students' progress. To do this you take into account what you know about science teaching and learning from your own experience, from local and national standards documents, and from discussions of student work with your peers. Once you've identified students' strengths and needs, you are able to adapt your teaching accordingly, and this cycle of reflection/assessment continues.

In this chapter we highlight the relationship between inquiry and continuous assessment. We describe the nature of inquiry, and how it simultaneously provides a rich context for formative assessment, and how using continuous assessment helps teachers facilitate inquiry more effectively.

WHAT IS INQUIRY?

The guidebook *Inquiry and the National Science Education Standards* (NRC, NAS, 2000) makes the point, "when educators see or hear the word 'inquiry,' many think of a particular way of teaching and learning science" (p. 13). That is:

> Inquiry is a multifaceted activity that involves making observations; posing questions; examining books and other sources of information to see what is already known; planning investigations; reviewing what is already known in light of experimental evidence; using tools to gather, analyze, and interpret data; proposing answers, explanations, and predictions; and communicating the results. Inquiry requires identification of assumptions, use of critical and logical thinking, and consideration of alternative explanations. (NSES, p. 23)

Inquiry is fundamental in the National Science Education Standards. It encompasses not only an ability to engage in inquiry but an understanding of inquiry and how inquiry results in scientific knowledge. "Scientific inquiry refers to the diverse ways in which scientists study the natural world and propose explanations based on the evidence derived from their work" (NSES, p. 23).

We refer to inquiry both as a way scientists (including children) work and come to learnings based on their questions and investigations, and also as a methodology for teaching and learning. Scientists (inside of and outside of the classroom) take actions based on the observations and findings of inquiry. They also use these findings to determine new questions to investigate.

The same is true when teachers take action based on the observations and findings they glean from their students. Continuous/formative assessment mirrors the inquiry process itself in that at each phase of inquiry, information can be collected, documented, and analyzed to determine the next steps of teaching and learning, and can be used to form the focus for the next round of observations.

The Foundation: Trust and Respect

> *"I knew that an important piece was treating the children's new discoveries with respect—allowing myself the time to catch their excitement by carefully listening to what they had to say, then asking my own questions, leaving the child to wonder . . ."*

> —First- and Second-Grade Teacher

Trust and respect for children as independent learners is the foundation of an inquiry approach. Inquiry-oriented teachers believe that their students come to the classroom with strongly held and well-developed (though not necessarily scientific!) ideas about the natural world. Teachers believe that students will eventually modify their ideas and construct an understanding closer to what is considered scientifically acceptable if they are given appropriate opportunities and challenges. To move to more sophisticated understandings of concepts, students need time and materials to actively explore their ideas and questions, opportunities to question and converse with teachers and peers, and a clear understanding of the learning goals of science.

You will find that when you engage with students from a foundation of trust and respect, the following practices work to engage students and support their learning:

- Uncovering students' ideas about the natural world and using these as starting points for investigations
- Using students' ideas as a baseline to monitor growth, and to adjust their inquiries
- Building on these ideas and setting up experiences, such as student-directed investigations and discussions, that guide students toward particular learning goals
- Inviting students to share their ideas, interests, questions, and suggestions throughout the investigative process
- Helping students make connections between their ideas/questions and their experiences both in and outside of school
- Helping students continually reflect on and acknowledge growth in their conceptual understanding and facility with science processes and dispositions over time

The Cycle of Inquiry

We suggest that thinking about inquiry in terms of a cycle helps us see more clearly the process scientists and students go through and the variety of activities they engage in as they explore phenomena and come to understand the natural world (see Figure 2.1). There are many ways to label the phases of such a cycle—the National Science Education Standards and many of the National Science Foundation–funded curricula include their own versions of a process for inquiry—but most describe the same phases in one way or another. These descriptions show how students engage in an inquiry, explore their ideas and questions about the concept, propose explanations and solutions, and take action/engage in further questioning and investigation.

- The initial phase, the way students come to engage in the inquiry, is described as an *invitation to learn*. Sometimes the invitation grows out of students'

Figure 2.1   In the Cycle of Inquiry

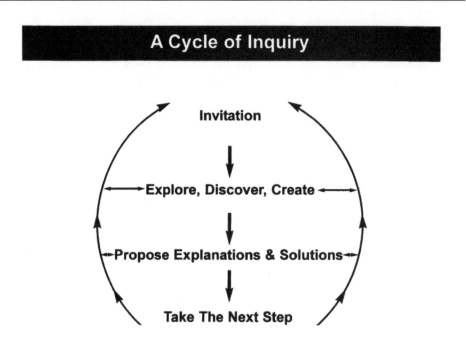

Adapted From:
Bybee, Rodger W., et al. 1989. *Science and Technology Education for the Elementary Years: Frameworks for Curriculum and Instruction.* The NETWORK Inc., Andover, MA: The National Center for Improving Science Education, 1989.

informal questions about and exploration of their world. Other times the invitation comes in a question you pose, a challenge you present, or an opportunity you set up for students to engage with specific materials related to a concept. In any case, students' curiosity is sparked and they want to "figure it out."

• In the *explore, discover, create* phase, students explore the question, the materials, and their ideas about the scientific phenomena presented to them. During this active phase, students may engage in focused play, investigate materials, collect and organize data, experiment, share their findings, and experiment further.

• As students *propose explanations and solutions,* they work to explain new views they've constructed about a concept based on their observations, their data, their peers' data, outside resources, and your input. This construction of knowledge occurs individually and through writing and/or conversation with peers and with you. In this phase new questions about their findings may arise, and you will want to provide your students with time to go back and retest some of their ideas.

• In the final phase, students consider how to extend their new understanding and skills, and *take next steps*. They may decide to try further explorations, address new questions, or seek to apply their knowledge to a new learning situation.

It is important to point out that although each stage in the cycle of inquiry is unique unto itself, the cycle is not a lock-step process. It is not a process that requires scripted science laboratory procedure and expects predetermined findings. Both on paper and in reality, the cycle of inquiry describes a much more fluid, dynamic process, one that reflects how science is done. Like scientists, students do not necessarily move through the cycle phase by phase. Students may be engaged in a particular phase of the learning process and then, because of a discovery or a new idea, cycle back to an earlier phase. For example, they may go through the *invitation to learn* phase, and the *explore, discover, create* phase, think of a new way to pose the question so that there is more clarity about what they're interested in, and start again. This starting and stopping, going in one direction and then changing course, is a natural and expected part of the scientific process.

At the same time, it is important for students to settle on one direction to move through and get to the latter stages of the cycle. You may notice that it is sometimes easy to think that you and the students are "done" with the investigation when they've finished the activity. Change in students' conceptual understanding comes when they work to make sense of their findings (*propose explanations and solutions*) and apply their understandings to new situations (*take next steps*). Like many teachers, you may find it challenging to support students to make these connections. While these are real challenges, they can be overcome. You may feel reluctant or unable to provide the time students need to wrestle with their ideas; however, the time you take with the students to make sense of their findings is as important as doing the activity itself. You might feel you need to better understand the concept yourself (which then will improve your ability to support students to fully understand it). This is where ongoing support and continued professional development helps and the payoff is real growth in students' understanding (see Chapter 6 for more detail).

What Does Inquiry "Look Like" in the Classroom?

So what does this look like in the classroom? How will you know if your students are "doing inquiry"? A group of elementary teachers working in a professional development initiative asked themselves the same question, and created the chart, *Inquiry/Standards-Based Science: What Does It Look Like?* (Figure 2.2). After experiencing science inquiry as adult learners, these teachers reflected on their work. They wanted to make a connection between what they were doing in this professional development initiative and what they might expect to see their students doing in science during the following year. Together they asked, "What were we doing that was good science?" "What did it look like?" and listed their ideas. They developed and categorized lists to capture the essence of their experiences. They carried forth this process and asked, "What would it look like in a classroom if students were similarly engaged in science inquiry?" and found many of their ideas to be the same as their experience. Comparing their ideas to local and national standards documents helped them to find any key components of inquiry they may have missed, and helped to assure them that their own ideas were supported by the national standards documents. In creating their personalized document, they found not only was it useful to help remind them what good standards-based science inquiry looks like, but it also helped to them to answer the question, "What would we be looking for when we assess our students?" *Inquiry Standards-Based Science: What Does It Look Like?* (Figure 2.2) then became a guide for the learning they ought to be facilitating as well as assessing.

The teachers' intent was to use the chart as a guide rather than as a checklist. Instead of placing a check mark (✓), they used the chart to remind them of the categories of evidence to document and annotate.

> *"When I'm planning a unit and thinking about what I want my students to learn, I pull out my Inquiry/Standards-Based Science chart. When I take notes or work with students to develop rubrics to document their experiences, I find myself using the language from the chart. I also find it useful to share with visiting parents, especially if the science time seems noisy and chaotic. I give parents a copy of the chart, explain what it is, then ask them if they notice any of the things happening in the classroom. It gives them something to do and helps them understand my science goals."*

—Second-Grade Teacher

> *"The 'IT' (the Inquiry/Standards-Based Science chart) was the most important thing for me. 'IT' gave me permission to do all the stuff I was doing. I didn't have anyone to team with so I would reread our statements and find guidance. It was like a person supporting me. Actually, I felt the power of all the people who created it supporting me."*

—Fourth-Grade Teacher

Figure 2.2 Inquiry/Standards-Based Science: What Does It Look Like?

Inquiry/Standards-Based Science

What Does It Look Like?

When students are doing inquiry-based science, an observer will see that:

Students view themselves as scientists in the process of learning.
They look forward to doing science.
They demonstrate a desire to learn more.
They seek to collaborate and work cooperatively with their peers.
They are confident in doing science; they take risks, display healthy skepticism, and demonstrate a willingness to modify ideas.

Students accept an "invitation to learn" and readily engage in the exploration process.
Students exhibit curiosity and ponder observations.
They take the opportunity and time to try out and persevere with their own ideas.

Students plan and carry out investigations.
Students design fair tests as a way to try out their ideas.
They plan ways to verify, extend, or discard ideas.
They carry out investigations by handling materials with care, observing, measuring, and recording data that will allow them to develop and evaluate their explanations.

Students communicate using a variety of methods.
Students express ideas in a variety of ways: through journals, reporting out, drawing, graphing, charting, and so on.
They listen, speak, and write about science with parents, teachers, and peers.
They use the language used by scientists to describe their approaches to explorations and investigations.
They describe their current thinking/theories about concepts and phenomena.

Students propose explanations and solutions and build a deeper understanding of science concepts.
Students offer explanations both from their previous experiences and from knowledge and evidence gained as a result of ongoing investigations.
They use and seek evidence to justify their own and others' statements.
They sort out information and decide what is important (what does and doesn't work).
They are willing to revise explanations and consider new ideas as they gain knowledge (build understanding).

Students raise questions.
Students ask questions (verbally or through actions).
They use questions that lead them to investigations that generate or redefine further questions and ideas.
Students value and enjoy asking questions as an important part of science.

Students observe.
Students observe carefully, as opposed to just looking.
They see details; seek patterns; detect sequences and events; notice changes, similarities, and differences.
They make connections to previously held ideas.

Students critique their science practices.
They create and use quality indicators to assess their own work.
They report and celebrate their strengths and identify what they'd like to improve.
They reflect on their work with adults and their peers.

Just as national committees discussed, revised, and solidified a statement of science education standards, this same type of discussion can happen on the local level. You as teachers with your students can engage in a similar process of clarifying and creating indicators for what is most valued in science teaching and learning. This process helps create a shared vision of the goals of science teaching and learning and prompts discussion about the nature of science and scientists. It enables you and your students to reach for, and *assess more deliberately* what is most valued. By making this vision public, you also enable parents, administrators, and the larger community to appreciate the nature and goals of good science teaching and learning, and to recognize when they are being achieved.

Planning for Equity in an Inquiry-Based Classroom

Being clear about what the standards are and what they look like in practice helps you plan learning opportunities for all students. Sometimes, some students "get it" sooner than others. Observing and noticing what students need on a day-to-day basis helps you reach out to those students who require more information or another technique to help them along. It also helps you to identify and help those students who might be ready to begin investigating the "next question" they have about their inquiry. You will begin to notice some of your own practices that are helpful in promoting equity and those that are out of balance. For instance, as you document information about your individual students, you may find that you frequently visit one group over and over again and you are not getting to other groups. You may find that you visit or call upon boys more than girls or vice versa. You can see how the way you have made up the student groups is working and be able to make adjustments when they are needed.

CONTINUOUS ASSESSMENT

Using Continuous Assessment Within a Cycle of Inquiry

Assessment in education has been criticized for interfering with the process of learning, the analogy being that of the gardener constantly pulling up plants to see if the roots are growing. There is some truth in this . . . but it also distorts reality to make a point. Gardeners do have to find out if their plants are growing and they do this, not by uprooting them, but by careful observation with a knowledgeable eye, so that they can give them water and food at the right times and avoid either under-nourishment or overwatering. . . . The gardener who does not know what size and shape a plant is to be and how quickly it is expected to grow will not know what signs to look for, and may mistake a condition which is quite normal for one which requires remedial action, or vice versa. We have to know something about the development taking place in order to interpret what we find when we assess it. (Harlen, 1983, p. vii)

So how can you assess students without uprooting them? Continuous assessment allows you to capture a wide range of evidence about your students while they are conducting and making sense of their investigations.

This is a unique feature of this type of assessment. At each phase of the cycle of inquiry, you are able to use continuous assessment techniques and tools to collect, document, and analyze information about your students and put your findings to use. You are able to look for indicators of growth in your students' science learning without interrupting them. What do students say in their discussions? What do their writings and actions reveal about their current understandings? Are their questions scientifically oriented? Can they set up a "fair test" to investigate a question? Can they observe carefully? Do they keep accurate records? Do they use their observations, discussions, and experiences to enrich and revise their theories? Do they give priority to evidence to develop and evaluate their explanations? Can they discuss ideas openly with their peers and build on others' thinking to further formulate and justify their explanations? Inquiry and continuous assessment have a mutual relationship. One benefits the other. As students construct their understanding through investigations over time, you can construct your understanding of students' growth over time through continuous assessment (see Figure 2.3).

Science inquiry leads to actions, and new questions come up for investigation based on your students' observations and findings; the same is true when you take action based on the findings you glean by observing your students. You can determine your next steps for teaching, and what the focus for your next round of observations of students will be. Continuous/formative assessment mirrors the inquiry process itself. In a sense, inquiry demands this type of formative assessment!

Some forms of assessment can give you slices of students' learning at a given point in time. For example, paper-and-pencil tests have the limitation of being able to show only what students can remember at that time, with an added challenge of students having to express what they know in a context and manner far removed from how they learned it in the first place. In another example, performance tasks can show you how students respond to a particular situation, and may give you information about where students are in their understanding at the time. Using continuous assessment strategies along with performance tasks and other forms of assessment allows you to know how students arrived at their understanding, and the range of scientific processes and dispositions students have demonstrated over the course of a long-term investigation.

Figure 2.3   Using Continuous Assessment Within a Cycle of Inquiry

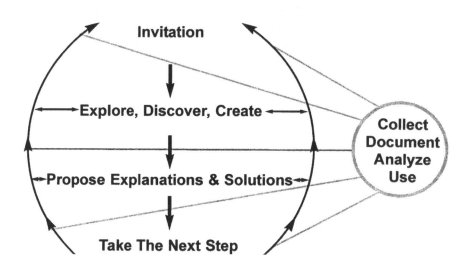

Adapted From:

Bybee, Rodger W., et al. 1989. *Science and Technology Education for the Elementary Years: Frameworks for Curriculum and Instruction.* The NETWORK Inc., Andover, MA: The National Center for Improving Science Education, 1989.

Just as gardeners need to have an image in their mind of what they expect their plants to look like and how they should behave throughout their growth cycle, you need to be clear about the concepts, processes, and dispositions you expect students to develop throughout the inquiry cycle.

Having this clarity will let you know what to plan, facilitate, and collect evidence of, and what to analyze to determine student growth.

> ### *What Should We Be Collecting Evidence Of?*
>
> Knowing What To Teach Is Knowing What to Assess
>
> What you believe is important about student learning in science is what you will look for when you assess. This vision is shaped by many factors: your own interests, your experiences with science as a learner and as a teacher, and local and national discussions about what is important for scientific literacy.

Having this clarity is the key factor in being able to make informed judgments and decisions. As one elementary teacher put it, "I know I'm supposed to be doing a unit on sound, but what exactly is it I want my students to learn?" How do you know what you want your students to learn?

Your state standards documents and district curriculum standards are good places to start to answer the question, "What should I teach, and therefore, what should I test?" Your local documents should be aligned with the *National Science Education Standards (NSES)*, NRC, and other widely used national documents such as the *Benchmarks for Science Literacy* (AAAS, 1993). As an indicator of how up-to-standards your curriculum materials, kits, and other teacher resource materials are, consider how well they are aligned with these Standards documents.

In the *NSES* you'll find summaries of the fundamental abilities and concepts that are needed to build scientific literacy in your students. These Standards promote a shift in expectations away from an emphasis on what has been considered traditional learning to more emphasis on understanding scientific concepts and developing the abilities of reasoning, critical thinking, and opportunities for communication.

See Resource B, Table B.2, "NSES: Changing Emphases for Contents," for a chart of NSES Content Standards that shows a shift in emphasis from older ideas to newer standards.

You will find that the content standards become more internalized as you use them both as goals to plan your students' activities and as targets for assessment. The more you use standards, the more you will become clear about what they are and the evidence to look for to determine if students are using them and growing in their understanding of them.

If you trust that students learn science best through doing science, and if you're interested in promoting and honoring students' growth in the processes and dispositions of science and conceptual understanding, you will want to assess their learning throughout their investigations. Student growth in these areas is ongoing. All of these goals of science learning are reached while students are fully engaged in their investigations and discussions. Why wait until the unit is finished before you start looking for evidence of learning?

Teaching and Continuous Assessment: Is There a Distinction?

Using continuous assessment also enhances your ability to facilitate inquiry. On the surface, it can seem like facilitating inquiry and using continuous assessment are the same thing. Your goal in using both processes is the same—to move students forward in their understanding of science concepts and their demonstration of science processes and dispositions. The actions can look the same, too—asking students a question is both a way to facilitate their inquiry and a technique of continuous assessment.

Trying to distinguish between facilitating inquiry and engaging in continuous assessment is a somewhat artificial process. In fact, some teachers might simply describe the approaches above as effective teaching. Our intent in raising this issue is to emphasize that beyond being ready and able to facilitate good learning opportunities, paying close attention to what students are saying and doing on an ongoing basis, and adjusting your teaching accordingly is the assessment aspect of this process. It is a powerful way to move students forward in both their conceptual understanding and their facility with scientific processes and dispositions. We'll talk more about specific tools and techniques you can use to do this in the next chapter.

Using Continuous Assessment Data

The analysis of the information you collect about your students will help you determine your students' needs and your own next steps. There are some situations that arise during investigations that might prompt you to reflect on your teaching and to adapt it. Some of these situations are fairly easy to identify. Providing a student group with a tool for measuring accurately, or giving information such as the order of the colors in a light spectrum may help the students' progress in their investigation. Other situations call for some quick decision making. Determining the best way to take students' learning deeper is one example. For instance, there are times when students' investigations and learning do not take the path that you or the curriculum developers had anticipated. This is the time for reevaluation! You can either make a decision to steer them back toward the planned results of the activity or you may consider adjusting your original plans to take advantage of an opportunity for learning brought up by a student's question or a group's findings. Another time, as you reflect on the day or watch a clip of a video you took during the class, you will find that you come up with a new way to approach the lesson so that there is more understanding by all of the students. This idea of analyzing and using the information you gather while paying close attention to students' ideas and ways of working will be more fully explored in Chapter 4.

Meanwhile, consider how a teacher of a multi-age first- and second-grade classroom uses continuous assessment within a cycle of inquiry as she and her students test the strength of magnets.

Vignette
Strength of Magnets

Mary sat with her multiage class of first and second graders. She was introducing them to some new materials to explore. They were simple materials, paperclips and small quarter-sized magnets. She was interested in having her students explore the concept of strength as a property of magnets. She was also interested is observing ways her students collected information about their investigations.

Invitation to Learn

The class began as the whole group sat in a circle and listened as Mary gave the directions. Mary challenged the students to attach a hook-shaped paperclip to one magnet, and see how many other clips they could hang on the hook before the holding clip fell off of the magnet. She asked them to predict what might happen. "What do you think?" she asked. "How many paperclips do you think the one magnet can hold? How many paperclips do you think two of the same kind of magnet will hold? Will two magnets hold more than one? How many think the two magnets will hold more? (hands are raised) How many think two magnets will hold about the same? (hands are raised again) How many of you aren't willing to take a guess yet and want to try it out?" (more hands are raised) Most of the children raised their hands to indicate they'd like to try it out before making a guess.

Reflection: Not only is Mary gathering information about what the children's ideas are before they start an investigation (assessment), but she is also trying to get the students to start thinking about their own ideas and how they might set up an investigation to test them out.

She urged the students to try the power of one magnet and get an idea about the strength of one magnet before going on to testing the strength of two magnets. At this time she showed the students how to use the science "jotters" she had made for them to record their results. Mary told the students that these "jotters" represented the science notebooks that scientists use. They were simply a piece of paper folded horizontally and then turned lengthwise so they could open like a book. The word "Magnets" was written at the top of the outside cover along with a space designated for the student's name and date. A question was printed on that outer cover: "How strong are magnets? What can you find out?" Inside the folded paper on the left was a heading, "Make a drawing." On the left side was, "Write a sentence," which the teacher explained to the students meant they could write something they found out during their investigation in that space. She urged the students to draw and write what they tried and what they

Figure 2.4   Hooked paperclip attached to a magnet, with two paperclips hanging

found out. When the students were in pairs, and two pairs were seated at an arrangement of four desks pushed together, she passed out a small tray to each group of four. The tray held a box of jumbo paperclips and four magnets for the students to share. Most groups work with no more than one partner.

Explore, Discover, Create

Many discoveries were made during their investigation.

Alicia and Kelsey had hooked their magnet to the metal leg of a desk. They didn't touch the magnet at all while they continued to add paperclips. At one point, the magnet started slipping down the leg of the desk. It slipped even more as more paperclips were added. One student with a slight disability was having trouble holding the magnet. She continued to hold the hooked paperclip to the magnet, rather than having it hang from the magnet by virtue of its attraction to the magnet. In doing it this way, the child found her clip could hold a massive amount of paperclips. Mary talked with this student, demonstrated how to hold the arrangement, and asked questions like, "What would happen if you moved your finger off of the hooked paperclip and tried letting it hang there by itself?" At first that didn't seem to help the child change her grip, until the child noticed her partner doing what Mary suggested. When she saw her partner follow Mary's instruction, she tried it herself. The surprise to Mary was that the massive amount of clips actually stayed there for a few seconds before slipping off!

After about 20 or 30 minutes of exploration, Mary called a scientists' meeting and told the children they could share their discoveries and ideas. She urged her students to put the paperclips back in the boxes and put the boxes and magnets back on the tray. One pair had made an arrangement with two magnets with a multitude of paperclips attached and asked Mary if they could hold on to it to show at the scientists' meeting. At Mary's instruction, the whole class spent about five or 10 minutes drawing and writing in their "jotters" before coming to the circle meeting.

Reflection: Mary explained that having the students write before they came to scientists' meetings, not only gave the students time to organize their ideas so they were ready to share; but the recordings they made on their scientist sheets gave Mary some data to look at and see what students tried and what they had found out. She would also use their writing as a starting point for conversations with the pairs when she went around the room, visiting pairs the next day.

Propose Explanations and Solutions

The theme of a "fair" way to hold the magnet ran throughout the discussion at the scientists' meeting. This conversation about "fairness" came up when Eric showed the group the arrangement of two magnets he and his partner had made with the multitude of paperclips attached. He was questioned by Michael as to whether the way he was holding the paperclip was a "fair test." Eric had found that putting the hooked paperclip between two magnets allowed him to attach many paperclips. Michael questioned the way Eric was holding the magnets and asked if he might be squeezing the two magnets together and thereby making them able to hold so many paperclips. Mary offered that she had the same question and encouraged Eric to arrange his fingers so that they were on the outside edges of the magnets instead of being on each side of the two magnets. Many of the students seemed surprised that the paperclips still held after Eric rearranged the way he was holding the two magnets. The question came up of whether the placement of the bent paperclip made a difference to how many paperclips could be held.

Michael and his partner were ready to try that investigation! They weren't themselves convinced yet about the arrangement Eric and his partner had made.

Reflection: Mary's response to this situation was quite unique. She considered the possibility of Eric's feeling accused if she told him he wasn't doing it right. She removed this possibility immediately when she instead showed honest curiosity herself and said she had the same question herself. Immediately the conversation turned toward interest in trying to figure out how Eric accomplished this instead of an accusation that he wasn't doing it fairly. As it turned out, Eric was being careful with how he held the arrangement, and the two magnets on either side of a paperclip apparently held a lot of paperclips! The fact that Mary suggested others might want to try Eric's idea tomorrow helped the students see that having skepticism is good, and a way for the students to resolve their question was to try it themselves.

Figure 2.5   Hooked paperclip between two magnets, with many paperclips hanging

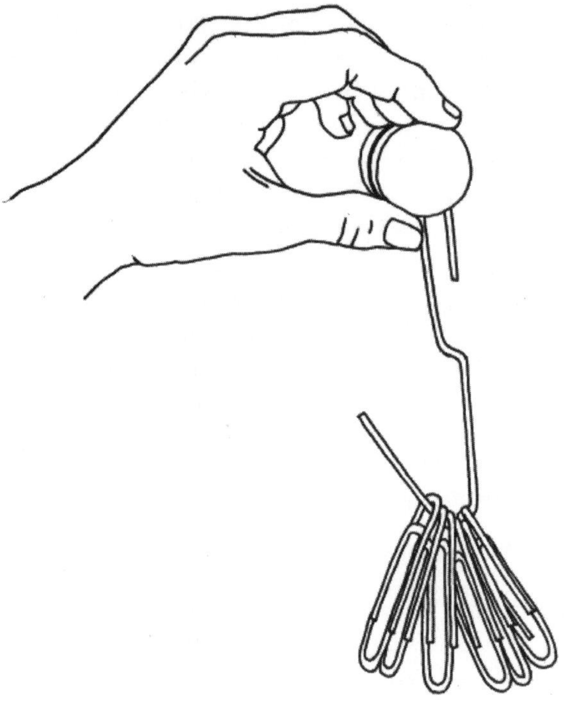

Take Next Steps

That was how the first day's session ended. At the end of the scientists' meeting Mary asked the students what they'd learned and what they'd like to do tomorrow. Some students reported that the magnets were stronger than they thought. Many students said they thought that two magnets would be stronger than one, but they wanted to try it out for themselves. Several students wanted to try the magnet on the leg of the chair as Alicia and Kelsey had done. Some students were ready to try three magnets! Mary kept track of their learnings and questions by listing them on chart paper with student names posted next to each contribution. She would use this chart the next day to prime the students' thinking about what they planned to investigate. She collected the "jotters" to quickly look over that night to see the ways the students recorded their data. Based on what she found, she might do a mini-lesson on drawing and writing about their findings.

Debriefing With a Peer

Mary had arranged for another teacher to videotape the investigation and the processing of ideas at the scientists' meeting. Mary and her colleague processed the tape after class. When it came to the section on the "sandwich magnet" Eric made, Mary's partner teacher noticed how Mary handled the discussion when she asked the students if the way they held the magnets made a difference in how "fair" the test was. She particularly noticed Mary's comment and how Mary also had the same question as Michael. Mary had diffused any potential arguments by saying that they were doing what scientists do when they challenge each other's data. Two girls were convinced that the "holder" clip would still be able to hold the large amount of paperclips. Mary encouraged them to try it out two more times and then call her back over when they were finished. The girls didn't get to the task by the end of class but kept the question to try out the next day.

The video clip was also helpful in terms of being able to see how the groups conducted their investigations. She noticed that one of the groups never showed up on the video, nor did she remember visiting with them during the class. Based on what she saw in the video, Mary decided to be sure to visit that group to check in on how they were progressing. She also decided which of the other groups she'd like to monitor for further help.

Reflection: In this case, debriefing and watching the videotape served as professional development for each of the teachers. Mary's partner teacher picked up on how Mary handled the overall discussion and in particular Mary's questioning skills. At the same time, Mary had someone to reflect with who was able to offer her feedback and listen to her ideas about the next day's class.

Content-rich, inquiry-based science teaching and learning is the context for the type of assessment we are discussing. It starts with the first question students and teachers have about the natural or technological world, and extends though planning and carrying out investigations, through discussions with their peers and with other science "experts." Students are building their abilities, and dispositions, critical thinking, and problem-solving skills to carry out and reflect on the results of their investigations. If science is all about asking questions, the processes of conducting and making sense of investigations, then why not capture evidence of students doing that and developing understanding while they work?

Techniques and Tools for Facilitating Inquiry and Collecting Student Data

3

H ow can you, the teacher, facilitate inquiry while simultaneously collecting data about each student's growth as a scientist? It may seem like a lot to juggle at one time, but in fact it is manageable with practice. This chapter describes techniques and tools that will help you both to facilitate inquiry and to continually assess student progress toward learning goals in science concepts, processes, and dispositions.

The first half of this chapter discusses continuous assessment techniques: sitting and listening closely, asking questions, sharing materials or information, sparking science conversations, and student self-assessment. These techniques are unique in that they not only help you assess where students are, but they are also ways that you can support students in their inquiries and move them forward in their thinking. In the second part of the chapter, we describe tools— teacher's observation notes, videotapes, audiotapes, photographs, student's science writing, and artifacts and products of student's science work—for gathering and recording evidence of student learning. You will recognize these tools and may already be familiar with them, but the way in which they are used may be new to your consideration. Also, both the techniques and the tools are not solely unique to science, but can be used in the assessment of many disciplines.

We chose to discuss the techniques and tools separately in this chapter to highlight the different facets of continuous assessment. While the distinct tools and techniques do exist, as you use them in the classroom you'll discover that they overlap and interweave. At times you may use a few techniques simultaneously (e.g., asking questions during a science conversation), or use a variety of techniques in a relatively short period of time. You may also document student learning with one of the tools at the same time you're using the techniques. For example, in a fifth-grade class, Mr. L decided to observe an investigation group he hadn't recently visited. He started by listening closely to the students' conversation in order to assess where they were in their investigation (technique: sitting and listening closely). During this time, he took notes about the group's progress (tool: teacher's observation notes). As he listened, Mr. L realized that the group had collected a lot of data and was struggling to make sense of it. In order to help them move forward, he suggested a data table to help them organize the data and look for patterns (technique: sharing a new material or piece of information). Once Mr. L was sure they understood how to use the data table, he left the group to organize their data on their own while he circulated to other groups. At the end of the session, he brought the students together in a scientists' meeting to discuss their investigations, and asked the group to share what they had learned as a result of their work with the data table (technique: sparking science conversations). Mr. L recorded this discussion on audiotape. On his way home, he listened to the audiotape in the car to gauge where students were in their investigations and, specifically, to check whether his suggestion had been helpful to that group (tool: audiotape). As a result of the information he heard, he decided to start class the next day with a review of the organization of data.

As you practice facilitating inquiry and continuous assessment, you'll develop a sense of how to choose techniques to best support student learning, and will find yourself transitioning naturally from one technique to another. Beginning with one technique or tool is the best way to get started. You'll soon discover which techniques and tools are most useful in your context for capturing the data you need.

TECHNIQUES FOR CONTINUOUS ASSESSMENT

- Sitting and listening closely
- Asking questions
- Sharing a new material or piece of information
- Sparking science conversations
- Student self-assessment

As teachers implement this approach, they often wrestle with what their role is as students are investigating. Many teachers find themselves spending a good deal of time running from group to group to assure that all students are on task, or searching the classroom for materials students have requested for their investigations (for more information about how to address challenges of materials management, see Chapter 6). While some time needs to be spent in these roles, the bulk of teacher time can be spent paying close attention to student learning. Continuous assessment techniques can help you be more intentional about this. The techniques are not new or unusual—teachers listen to students and ask them questions every day. What's different about using these techniques to facilitate inquiry and continuous assessment is the intent— that you are consciously using the techniques to inform your instruction, enhance student learning, and/or gather information about your teaching. On the surface, this can sound overwhelming, but over and over again, teachers report how fascinating it is to really listen to students and strive to understand their thinking. They relate how rewarding it is to find ways to move them forward in their understanding. This is the essence of continuous assessment—a continual curiosity about and intense interest in what students are doing and saying, how they're progressing in their learning, and how your teaching is affecting this. Curiosity and a "desire to know" are also key components of inquiry. You model these important scientific dispositions as you seek to better understand students' learning.

Sitting and Listening Closely

"When I first tried listening quietly and taking notes about what I heard students saying as they worked, my insight into their learning was phenomenal! I actually stopped talking and just listened. The data I collected showed some incorrect conceptions as well as understanding. It often opened windows into how a student had learned. The rich data I gathered helped me determine which next steps I needed to take to further learning."

—Third-Grade Teacher

At times, you may choose to observe quietly and listen closely as your students plan, carry out, and construct meaning from investigations. You might ask questions to clarify what students are doing and/or saying, but otherwise not interfere. This noninteractive time provides you the opportunity to record and reflect on students' thinking as they're working productively on their own. It also sends a message to students about the importance and integrity of their independent work, and about your confidence in their ability to grapple with their own understanding without your guidance (an important part of building a classroom culture that supports inquiry).

There are many situations in which you might want to sit and listen closely for a while before using any of the other techniques. This can be challenging at first. Your instinct might be to direct the learning in some way, to make sure that you are actively supporting student learning. Sometimes, though, your interaction with students can get in the way of their learning:

> *"A group of children was working diligently to move water between two tubs by using turkey basters and eyedroppers. As they worked, I fired away with questions: 'Do the turkey basters and eyedroppers all work the same? Are some of them easier to move water with than others? How do they work?' Within minutes I had asked seven questions! Most of the group, appropriately, had ignored me. At times, I need to remember that I can best support inquiry without saying a word."*

—Elementary Teacher

Following are situations when it is helpful to listen closely and gather information before employing any of the other techniques:

- When students are working productively on their own
- When you first approach a group you haven't seen for awhile
- In the early stages of an investigation when students are messing around with materials for the first time and haven't formed a lot of ideas/questions yet
- When students are working hard to figure something out (and are making progress) and where your telling them would take away the chance for them to discover it themselves

As you observe and listen to your students, you may also want to employ one of the tools (e.g., note taking, videotape, audiotape) to document what's happening. If students are in the early stages of the investigation, you might want to note their understanding of a concept and/or their misconceptions. If they are struggling with something, you might note the nature of the struggle and any ideas you have for helping them out should they not be able to work it out on their own. If it's later in an investigation, you might want to capture evidence that shows changes in students' conceptual understanding since the beginning of the unit, and/or their use of science processes and their demonstration of scientific dispositions.

> *"The most powerful strategy for my own development as a teacher, and for the students as learners, was sitting close and listening. By keeping notes and reflecting on what I heard, I moved to the next step."*

—First- and Second-Grade Teacher

Asking Questions

In *Primary Science . . . Taking the Plunge* (Harlen, 1985), Jos Elstgeest provides a structure for appropriate questioning by describing the difference between "productive" and "unproductive" questions. He illustrates how inappropriate questions focus a child's thoughts on finding someone else's "right" answer. These unproductive questions require recall of predetermined right answers, and prevent students from using their own logical thinking skills. Without a connected web of experiences or ownership of the learning process, facts become isolated, useless bits of information that are soon forgotten. In contrast, Elstgeest describes productive questions as those that stimulate active inquiry and observation, and encourage students to seek their own solutions.

> *"Children began to hear me asking, 'What do you notice about the inside of a pumpkin?' or 'Can you find a way to make the car go down the ramp faster?'"*
>
> —Elementary Teacher

When you ask questions that provoke students to reflect on, clarify, and explain their thinking and actions, you gain insight into their understanding and reasoning. In doing so, you also model the type of discourse that students can have with one another. If this approach is new to you, it can be challenging to know what question to ask and when. Teachers experienced in facilitating inquiry and continuous assessment suggest starting by trying to figure out what students are doing and thinking, perhaps by simply saying, "Tell me what you're doing." Then as students talk with you, you can ask clarifying questions about their inquiry, their process, and their findings to date. Again, if you're genuinely curious about students' thinking, you'll find that your questioning will come out of your desire to understand.

Some teachers find it helpful to post a list of productive question starters in the classroom to guide their questioning of students and students' questioning of one another. Other teachers prefer to carry a list of questions on a clipboard as they circulate among investigation groups. Here are some examples of open-ended questions that you can ask as students are engaged in the different phases of science explorations:

- What have you tried so far?
- What do you think will happen if . . . ?
- Can you find a way to . . . ?
- What are you thinking about?

- I'm wondering what you meant when you said . . . ?
- Can you tell me why you decided to. . . ?
- Can you tell me more about . . . ?
- Why do *you* think it happened that way?
- How would *you* explain . . . ?
- What questions do you have now?

> *"Because questioning can either promote or stifle discussion, I have been working on asking 'productive' questions and allowing students "think time" before answering. I am asking more 'What would happen if . . .?' questions. Instead of just asking 'why?' I am trying to ask, 'Why do **you** think . . . ?' questions that will elicit the students' thinking process. The 'why?' questions can intimidate the students because they are more hesitant to share an answer that they think may be wrong."*

—Fifth-Grade Teacher

It is important to note the critical role questioning plays in helping students make sense of their investigations. To move students forward in their thinking, you need to know what they understand about the concepts. Often students can repeat back to you things they've read in books, heard you say, or "know" from other experiences, without really understanding the concepts behind the words. You might ask a few questions, hear some scientific words, and assume your students have the ideas. If you want to be sure your students grow conceptually, talk with students about their investigations. Ask them often to clarify what they mean, especially if they are using concept-related vocabulary. Keep probing until you're sure you know what they understand. Often you'll find that students are clear about some ideas and still working with others. This important assessment data can help you think about what you might do in the next days or weeks to help students fill in the gaps in their thinking.

Sharing a New Material or Piece of Information

At times, students can become "stuck" in investigations and not know where to go next, or can be led by inaccurate data or lack of sufficient knowledge/skills to erroneous conclusions. You can help students move forward in their thinking and skills by sharing a particular material or piece of information. For instance, if your first-grade students have created an "our heights" chart that does not accurately reflect the heights of children in the class, you might ask them why they think that happened. As they show you how they measured, you may discover you need to teach students how to identify starting and ending points for measuring. Or if your third-grade students aren't noticing subtle changes in their ailing plants because they aren't observing closely, you might do a mini-lesson on observing details so that students can better identify, understand, and try to correct the problem. There may also be times when it is appropriate to supply important content information to help students move forward with conceptual understanding. For example, your sixth-grade students are exploring sinking and floating. They collect data about the weights and volumes of the objects, and are speculating that these properties have something to do with whether objects sink or float, but can't figure out the relationship. Knowing they are on the verge of a discovery, you share with them that 1 ml of water = one gram and therefore the density of water is 1.0 g/cm^3. You then suggest that they organize their data by sinkers and floaters, and notice the relationship of the volumes and weights of these objects to the density of water.

How you share such information or materials should also be a deliberate decision. If students are stuck, you may first want to ask how they're doing, and let the request for help come from them. If students aren't aware that they're stuck or that their conclusions are incorrect, you might simply present the material or information and suggest that it might help them in their work. Then if students don't take advantage of the offering, you can question them or make a suggestion to help them get back on track. You also can draw on students to help each other move forward. For instance, if you notice that a group has used materials or information to further their thinking, you might ask them to share their ideas in a scientists' meeting to benefit others. Other groups can then turn to this group for support as they try out the suggestions.

Again, being clear yourself about the concepts, processes, and dispositions you want your students to learn will help you to know what material or information you might share. It is also helpful to understand what misconceptions are common for students at your grade level, and what is reasonable to expect in terms of conceptual development and skill use. The National Science Education Content Standards and Project 2061's Benchmarks and Atlas of Scientific Literacy are good resources for this information. With this knowledge, you can more clearly gauge students' emerging understanding and skill development, and decide how to help them to move forward.

Sparking Science Conversations

Students' understanding will unfold and deepen as they grapple with concepts and data, defend their own views, and listen to others' perspectives. Whether with peers or with you, these conversations are a natural part of your students' process as they plan, carry out, and try to make sense of their investigations. They also provide you with valuable data about students' progress toward learning goals.

There may also be times when you'll plan a discussion for a particular purpose. For instance, you might ask groups to share their investigation plans with each other during a scientists' meeting. Getting feedback and new ideas from their peers can help students develop and improve upon their plans while "doing what scientists do." Not only do these discussions help provide feedback and new ideas, they also provide a context for you to gather data about students' planning abilities and their understanding of the inquiry process. Alternatively, you might interview individuals or small groups to determine their understanding of a concept. In this way, this technique helps you both gauge and challenge students' thinking. Consider the following contexts for conversations:

- Brainstorming sessions with individuals, investigative groups, or the whole class
- Whole-class or small-group "scientists' meetings" during which students exchange thoughts, ask questions about concepts or investigations, and demonstrate and discuss intriguing investigative findings
- Discussions of video clips, audiotape excerpts (or transcripts), or photographs of students conducting investigations
- Oral or written conversations about students' journal entries
- Teacher and peer conversations about products and presentations sparked by student investigations

Student Self-Assessment

As noted in Chapter 2, respect for students and what they bring to the learning situation is a key component of inquiry. Teachers practicing inquiry and continuous assessment support students' taking as much responsibility for their own learning as is developmentally appropriate. Just as students can learn to work independently in investigation groups, they can learn to assess their own and their peers' learning. Engaging students in self-assessment contributes to their investment in the learning process and to their ability to work independently. Perhaps more important, however, when done effectively, it can enhance student learning.

There are three things that students need to understand in order for their self-assessment to be successful in furthering their learning: the learning goals (what is expected of them), where they are in their conceptual understanding and/or practice of skills and dispositions, and how to close the gap (Black & Wiliam, (1998, p. 144). If you practice continuous assessment, you and your students will have all this information. As you plan a science unit, you consider what you want students to learn in terms of science concepts, processes, and dispositions, focusing on just a few at a time so you'll have the time to go into depth. You share these learning goals with students, so they know what you're looking for and what they need to work on. In continuous assessment, students participate in assessment with you—they are an integral part of the process. As students engage in activities and investigations, you help them to use continuous assessment techniques to see where they are, and to challenge their thinking in order to move themselves forward. You encourage them to use the tools of continuous assessment to document their progress. This, along with the documentation you are collecting, can be shared and is another way for them to reflect on and deepen their learning.

> *"I have always felt that our students have a lot to tell us about their own learning if we as teachers could just listen. We need to be able to hear the children's voices, and distill what they are trying to tell us about themselves."*

> —Fifth-Grade Teacher

TOOLS FOR CONTINUOUS ASSESSMENT

- Teacher's Observation Notes
- Videotape
- Audiotape
- Photographs
- Student Science Writing
- Products of Student Science Work

As you observe and interact with students using the techniques described above, you'll have rich opportunities to document their thinking, abilities, and dispositions. Teachers have found that the tools for documentation described in this section, used individually and in combination with the techniques, can provide compelling records of students' science work. Once again, you may already be using many of these tools in your classroom. In this chapter we offer suggestions about how to use them to further the collection of data for decision making, for taking learning deeper in the present, and for summative purposes at various times throughout the school year.

To begin, start small. Choose one tool and try it in several different situations to see what you can learn about your students. Which tool you choose may depend on your experience and comfort with it, the resources available to you, and which aspects of a science session you want to capture.

Also, don't feel like you need to capture every student each day. At first you may find it uncomfortable not collecting information on every student each day. Choose to focus on just a few students at a time, and consider what you can learn about them as individuals. What you will find is that what you learn about a few will tell you a great deal about the class as a whole.

If the first tool you choose doesn't work for you, try another. You don't need to master every one; instead, find one or two that are manageable and provide you with the information you need about your students and your teaching. The point is not to become an expert on documentation, but rather, an expert (over time) on each of your students. Routinely using the tools can help you to "learn to see"—to develop the *habit* of paying close attention to what your students think, say, and do every day and to put that information to work.

As noted in the discussion of the techniques, you may be amazed at what you discover about your student scientists as you document what they

> The point is not to become an expert on documentation, but rather, an expert (over time) on each of your students.

say and do. This may be a significant "aha" for you, yet your documentation will take on a much greater meaning if you take the time that day or before your next science session to reflect on your data and act on what you learn (for more information on how to analyze the data you collect, see Chapter 4). This cycle of observation, documentation, reflection, action, and observation—*while* you and your students are engaged in teaching and learning—is at the heart of continuous assessment. It is one of the features that differentiates it from more summative forms of assessment like tests.

Tool 1: Teacher's Observation Notes

"At the beginning of the year, I would sit quietly and observe children investigating, trying to capture the whole of what was happening. Students were fascinated by my stand-back position. They wanted to know what I was doing and how it related to them personally, and they wanted me to 'get it right.' So we began the 'write and share' conference mode. Before I left a group I'd been observing, I would refer to my notes and do a 'mini-share' of what I had heard. It gave me the opportunity to probe student thinking, and students had a chance to clarify things they had said. One time I heard a student questioning her peers and recording on a clipboard what others were saying. I asked what she was doing and she said that everyone in her group was making lots of good connections that I wasn't there to record, so she was doing it for me!"

—Third-Grade Teacher

Many teachers tell us that they use notes to record their observations as they sit and listen closely to students. They document and generate records of their students' words, ideas, and actions. They also record their interpretations of what happens as students investigate. These notes help teachers make immediate and long-term instructional decisions, and provide documentation for later use in summative reporting. With practice, teachers include in their notes judgments about students' progress in understanding of science concepts, practice of science processes, and demonstration of the dispositions of science.

At first you may find it challenging to take notes while you are facilitating students' investigations. Sometimes teachers get overwhelmed in trying to write down everything they see, or trying to record notes for every child. Instead, before you begin a note-taking session, consider your goals for the session. Whenever possible, decide ahead of time whether you will track selected students or a particular learning goal.

"What I have found works the best is to choose a specific focus and write to it for a particular note-taking session. For instance, at the beginning of the year, or at the beginning of a new science unit, I like to watch how students 'dive into science.' I write down what I can on individual students as they first tackle an investigation. I watch for the use of particular processes and note strengths and weaknesses. I can revisit this same idea later on in the year and compare notes over time."

—Fourth-Grade Teacher

After considering your purpose, determine the materials and structure you will use to accomplish your goals: a blank piece of paper, sticky-notes or computer labels for each student, and/or an observation form. There are sample formats for structuring observation notes on the following page, but you may also want to design a note-taking form that will help you better achieve your goals. To be effective, structured forms need to allow adequate space for you to record evidence of students' demonstrating their understandings and skills. Forms that allow only a checkmark beside a skill or concept do not give you that important information. Try to record pure observations (what you saw/heard) as well as your impressions and interpretations of what you saw/heard.

In addition to the times when you want to focus in on a particular concept, skill, or disposition, there will be times when you will want to be open to the variety of information that might present itself. Avoid becoming so focused on your note-taking goals that you overlook opportunities that come up while students are working. You might hear the all-important "aha" of a student who suddenly understands a concept. Even if that student is not the focus of that day's note taking, take time to record some notes about that student's growth as well.

> "As my note-taking skill progressed, I began to focus on certain students each day. This got complicated because students often asked me to come and record what they had just discovered. I found I had to keep a student list and record or check off whom I had worked with on a daily basis and schedule those that I had missed for the following days."
>
> —Third-Grade Teacher

Whenever possible after a note-taking session, take time to organize and review your observation notes. Consider ways you might improve your use of this tool. In addition to the rich data they provide, your written observations can provide excellent jumping-off points for individual and whole-class discussions.

Samples of Note-Taking Formats

Figure 3.1 shows some possible formats for structuring your observation notes. Remember, the format needs to work for you, so feel free to make changes to fit your needs or to create your own.

Tool 2: Videotape

> "The videotaping worked out very well, and the camera has become a familiar sight to the children. They continue their work, and discuss their thoughts with me, unfazed by the sight of this silly apparatus in front of my face. Occasionally, a child requests that I capture on tape a special event."
>
> —Kindergarten Teacher

Video technology offers a powerful tool for documenting student learning as inquiry occurs because it captures so many dimensions of classroom activity: the setting; the students' actions, interactions, and words; and your conversations and movement in the room. You can view, review, and analyze the images more than once, which allows you to see and learn more than you can through your own observations.

Figure 3.1   Sample Formats for Structuring Observation Notes

Record sheet using sticky labels

Light Investigations..... 4/4/03
Jill...............................
Sue......................
Mark...............

Activity Focus _____ Date _____	
Observation Notes	Reflections on Notes

Record sheet for your observations with space for comments/reflections

Record sheet for annotating evidence of students' ideas and practice

Name/ Date	Asking Questions	Testing Ideas	Proposing Explanations	Revising Explanations
Mary 01/17	She asks, "What will happen if we put one ice balloon in the light and one in the dark?"	Fair test . . . used the same size and shape balloon	Seems to be equating 'heat' with light	
Sam 01/07	Chose to work on another student's question. Can he raise his own?			
Kera 01/19	Good! Does it matter if the ice melts on Styrofoam or aluminum?		Thinks ice on Styrofoam melts slower	

A video record is immediate and compelling to students, which makes it a powerful instructional tool. (When you use a video camera frequently, your students will accept it as just another item in the classroom—you don't have to worry about it distracting them from their inquiry.) Try spending time with your class reviewing selected clips from the tape and inviting students to discuss what was happening in the images. Stop the tape from time to time to freeze the frames and ask the students what they were thinking and doing, and what they might do to test new ideas or move farther with their inquiry. This kind of reflection deepens student understanding and it simultaneously helps you learn more about where your students are, and the next steps you can take to help them progress toward learning goals.

> *"The best strategy that I've used to document and make sense of science learning has been videotaping science experiences, revisiting them by watching clips with students, then interviewing them about what they initially experienced and thought about when they viewed the tape of them doing science."*
>
> —Elementary Teacher

Reviewing videotapes of science inquiry also can help you reflect on your teaching. Look to see how much time you spend interacting meaningfully with groups compared to how much time you spend as a removed observer or disciplinarian. Are your interactions with students moving them forward or interfering with their process? How can you better facilitate learning? Ask a colleague to watch a video clip with you and comment on particular issues about your teaching that you wish to address. You will be surprised by how much you both learn!

> *"Listening carefully to videotaped conversations helps me to understand how questions can extend conversations or interrupt children's work. Since communication is more than just the spoken word, the visual images provide additional feedback about the effectiveness of various questioning strategies.*
>
> —Kindergarten Teacher

When you use your videotapes as a permanent record of the evolution of student learning, you can revisit them to see how students' thinking and skills have developed over time. You can also use these tapes to share the process of inquiry with other teachers, administrators, and parents who are curious about how students are growing and changing through their science investigations.

"We used it after an investigation of the question, 'What is the most effective way to empty water from a two-liter soda bottle?' This was a great warm-day activity to do outside. Seeing themselves on the television monitor helped them to settle down and become focused when we reentered our classroom, not to mention the good discussion that took place as a result of revisiting their investigations by means of the digital photographic slide show."

—First- and Second-Grade Teacher

Tool 3: Audiotape

"The majority of my students felt that they best communicated their science learning through conversations with other students. In response to that, the students and I needed to find ways to capture that learning. We needed to challenge ourselves to document the science talk that occurred while students were engaging in inquiry. The audiotape allowed us to capture that conversation."

—Fifth-Grade Teacher

In the inquiry classroom, children learn science by exploring materials, articulating and discussing their thoughts with peers and teacher, testing new ideas, and revising their views. The conversations that occur as students investigate are instrumental to their developing new ideas and provide you with a window into student thinking and learning. Listening carefully to these conversations is an essential form of continuous assessment.

"The dialogue that took place while two students were involved in an investigation was different from the dialogue that occurred between teacher and student. Both of those dialogues were valuable and they each provided different types of information."

—Fifth-Grade Teacher

With so many students simultaneously engaged in inquiry throughout the classroom, it is difficult to hear all that occurs. Tape recorders placed on the tables of working groups can help you address this challenge by recording the conversations of investigation groups you might not get to in a session, and/or groups you know are able to work independently. Carrying a tape recorder with you to document the conversations you have with students allows you to gather data and reflect on your teaching. Recording whole-class science meetings gives you a chance to reflect on the progress of the class as a whole and the efficacy of your teaching, and provides documentation of students' understanding at that point in time. As with each piece of technology, there will be challenges and discoveries that come with repeated use of the tool.

"One day I decided to set up a tape recorder during the science unit. The problem was that we were working with magnets, so of course I couldn't put it right in the middle of things. The voices were pretty hard to hear because I'd put the recorder off to the side. It might not have been the best tool for this particular unit, but the next time I'll put it in an area where it's not blocked from the kid's voices. But I tried anyhow, and I learned something from that. The next time I tried the recorder, I used it to back up my notes on what the students were saying. That worked out well because I knew if I didn't get it all, I didn't have to panic because I knew it would be on my tape."

—Kindergarten Teacher

Some teachers find a quiet time to review the tapes while commuting or exercising. As you listen to the audiotapes, you will hear what students are thinking and how well they understand and can use scientific terms. Selecting portions of the tape to share with your students is a way to spark conversations and help determine next steps in the inquiry. Portions that you wish to focus on can be transcribed (by you, by volunteers, or by aides) for use with students or for your reflection and for permanent records. Transcribing is time-consuming, so transcribe only those segments of the conversation that give you the most information.

Tool 4: Photographs

"When we take time to take pictures of children, listen to their words, transcribe those words, then bring them back and share them with the class and others, we send children the clear messages that what they do is really important. So children feel pretty special since somebody's paying so much attention to their work. It's so important that I am going to take pictures, write down their words, and that we'll talk about them as a class. It creates a classroom culture that is very respectful of all of us."

—Kindergarten Teacher

Many teachers already use photography in their classroom to capture images of students engaged in learning. Many times, however, the pictures are pinned on the bulletin board or slipped into a child's folder. In the inquiry classroom, photography can be used to track growth in students' scientific ideas and skills. By periodically snapping photos of your students at significant moments in their work and using these images as fuel for further learning, you can help students explore new directions in their inquiry and deepen their conceptual understanding.

One way to use photos is to ask students to identify the science processes and dispositions they're exhibiting in each photo. You may want to structure a time for students to write about the images you collect. Asking students to write immediately following that day's inquiry time is often effective. Prompt them to write about what was happening and what they were doing or thinking at the time of the photo. Revisiting the photo and their writing can lead to a discussion of how their ideas have changed, and what new questions they have. These student writings and corresponding photographs can help document the evolution of students' conceptual understandings, processes, and dispositions throughout the investigation.

"I do a lot of photo taking so I can have pictures to match with quotes of what kids said during investigations so the students can later reflect on what they'd been thinking and doing. They're also useful to post in the hall so parents and others can see what science looks like in the classroom. When one student was trying to experiment with the 'bendability' of bark (as we explored why certain Native Americans used birch bark for canoes), I took a couple of pictures as she experimented. I knew conceptually that part of her experiment wouldn't work, and wanted to have a record so she could revisit and discover that on her own. When we later conferenced with the photos in front of us, I was able to ask her questions based on what she'd been trying at the time I captured her on film. As she looked back at the photos, she was able to see and reflect on why some ideas might not work. Sometimes, if students are having trouble in an investigation, I might say, 'Can you look at your picture and see what you might do differently if you were to test it again?' Most kids find it much easier when they're reflecting on whether a test was fair or on results, to have a photo as a reminder of what actually transpired."

—Third-Grade Teacher

You might also bring these photos to whole-class science meetings and use them to spark discussions, for example, by asking, "What was happening in this photo that demonstrates good science?" Students love reflecting on the important moment that was captured on film, and these class discussions can help your class jointly determine next steps to take in the inquiry. As the unit concludes, invite students to use the photos as part of final products and presentations.

When you use the camera as a documentation tool, it is helpful to have the students annotate each photo as soon as possible after it is taken. Inviting students to annotate photos taken of them as they work will help them reflect on their learning and on the value of their science inquiry activities. It also brings more writing into the curriculum. The same is true for the teacher.

Write notes in a photo journal if using 35 mm photography, on the computer if using digital photography, and on the bottom of the photograph if using Polaroid technology. What was the student(s) doing? What skills and understandings was the student displaying? What difficulties was the student having? How can you help that student progress? Recording evidence of science knowledge, processes, and dispositions displayed in the photo will help you consider what next steps to take to help the student move forward in the investigation.

"I feel that with a Polaroid or digital camera in hand, the teacher becomes the researcher, snapping a picture of an excited moment, then following this up with specific questions, such as: 'What were you doing when this happened? Why do you think it went this way? Can you make it happen again?' (This is a good question for those times that you weren't actually right there to photo-document the moment.)

"However, just snapping the picture is not enough to really be called assessment. The next step is to jot some notes, label the picture in a way that points out specific connections to what is valued in terms of developing processes, concepts, and dispositions of science, and identify the students involved, perhaps specifying who said or did what. It is actually this journaling piece complementing the photograph that creates a valid assessment document. When students view and discuss the photographs, their reflective comments strengthen the ongoing assessment process."

—Sixth-Grade Teacher

Today, three different types of cameras are useful continuous assessment tools: standard 35 mm, Polaroid, and digital. In addition, scanners can be used to create digital images from photographs. Using Polaroid or digital cameras instead of 35 mm cameras can minimize the time lapse between shooting and developing. If your classroom has access to digital technology and computers, you can combine the photographic and written portions of your documentation to create a journal in progress. Students can also use digital photographs to illustrate computer presentations detailing their explorations and their progress toward learning goals.

"The children love to see themselves in action and often ask if a picture can be taken to document an activity that is important to them. In this case, I am given another opportunity to ask the children specific questions, and

probe their thinking. At parent conferences, the photos are concrete evidence that the children were happily involved in their work.

"The photographs allowed the children to recall an activity and to talk and write about what they were doing, telling what they noticed about themselves and their science investigation. Their writing allowed us another avenue to get at their thinking.

—First- and Second-Grade Teacher

Tool 5: Students' Science Writing

Before, during, and after investigations, scientists write down their observations and questions as they reflect on their findings and determine next steps. Students are scientists when they do the same.

Writing is one of the most powerful tools for encouraging self-reflection and building understanding. Many elementary school teachers already use journals in a variety of subject areas. In science, journals or notebooks can help students learn to articulate their thoughts and convey their understanding of scientific phenomena. Students may write observations, draw pictures and/or diagrams, and pose questions in a notebook while they investigate, and then reflect on their explorations at the end of a session or unit. This student writing is another window into science learning and an effective tool for continuous assessment.

"While the children wrote and drew, I'd go around and ask them about what they were thinking. I jotted down their responses on a sticky note, which I attached to their journal page. The journal became an instrument for the child to help collect and record observations for self-reflection.

"A child made the following journal entry early in second grade after messing about with cornstarch and water: 'When I felt it, it felt like glue. And when I held it, it washed out.' I asked her what she meant by 'washed out.' She told me, 'It dissolved when I washed my hands.' I wrote what she told me on a sticky note and handed it to her to put on her journal page. I hoped that my notes to the children helped to model how they could use their journals to help keep track of and document experiences. I found her use of the word 'dissolved' to be interesting, and this reflection time allowed her to be ready to share with the group. The discussions which resulted from their writing were filled with the use of vocabulary words which came from the students and which generated a host of responses

when students were asked to tell us what they meant by a particular word.
Many private conceptions and hypotheses, along with further questions to
investigate, came from this discussion time."

—First- and Second-Grade Teacher

Many teachers find that using science notebooks in different ways works
well for different children. Students can use their notebooks as "jotters"
to record observations, questions, diagrams, drawings, and ideas *during* the
investigation. These are quick notes to help the students remember details
of the investigations. On the other hand, there are times when students
might use their notebooks more as a "journal" to reflect on and react to their
experiences in a quiet time *after* the investigation. During this time, you can
pose questions to elicit discussion of students' ideas. Questions such as,
"What did you learn today?" "What are you thinking about as a result of
today's investigation?" or, "What will you try next?" move students away
from spending time describing in detail what they did, to what their findings
and learnings are.

"The kids were involved today with building layers of fluids as a way to
look at density. Several years ago if I had been doing this I would have
had the kids journaling as they worked. What I found is that sometimes
the journaling wasn't that focused, so I evolved to having kids work
with the materials first and write afterward. They reflect and think
about what they've done, and try to pick one or two moments to really
consider in their journal entry. This is more effective than journaling as
they go."

—Sixth-Grade Teacher

When you offer students an opportunity to converse privately with you
about their writing, you gain further insight into what each one is learning. For
less outgoing students, this private conversation is especially important, as it
allows them time and space to share their ideas with you. For students who are
not developmentally ready for writing, talking with you while you transcribe
helps assure the child that what she or he wants written is recorded.

Many teachers find it useful to hold a class meeting after journal writing, or
first thing the next science session. Having just written about them, students
can more easily share their experiences, thoughts, and questions, and you can
gain valuable information from the class as a whole about where they are in
their investigations.

"Talking about science data and ideas [documented in journals] was critical in shaping and expanding these ideas. I found that our scientists' meetings led to the construction of science knowledge and often pushed the children's thinking and changed random explorations into more focused investigations. Listening closely to what the children say often helps me to plan the 'next steps' for students' exploration within a specific unit."

—Fourth-Grade Teacher

Advances in technology make it easy to produce many creative documents to demonstrate student learning. As we have previously said, asking students to combine digital images and writing to describe the evolution of their thinking helps get at their most current understanding of the concepts.

"This year our school purchased a digital camera. We take photos of kids investigating, and put those on the computer, with space at the bottom for kids' writing. Lots of times kids know what they want to say, but have a difficult time writing it down. The photograph gives these students a way to observe themselves in action. Their writing is more descriptive than when it's on a blank page, and sometimes even better than with their own drawing because they're able to observe things captured in a still picture that were happening sometimes very quickly. It's a continuation of trying to offer kids opportunities to sit back and reflect on what they are doing as a way to make some insights that they didn't see right at the time."

—Sixth-Grade Teacher

Tool 6: Artifacts and Products of Student Science Work

The cycle of inquiry presents your students with an opportunity to generate artifacts and products that offer powerful insight into your students' conceptual understanding, use of science processes, and demonstration of science dispositions. Be ready to collect, and reflect on this evidence as part of your continuous assessment documentation.

Artifacts are concrete objects. Drawings, diagrams, and models are examples of artifacts that can be used for continuous assessment. Whenever appropriate, ask your students to create visual images of their investigations as they are working. Encourage them to diagram and label their materials set-up, the methods that they used to explore the materials, or the outcomes of their investigations. These artifacts become especially useful as you discuss portions of the investigation that you "missed" when you were working with another group.

Products are not as tangible as artifacts, but still can be recorded and stored as another useful tool for continuous assessment. Student demonstrations are one example of a product that can be assessed. Consider taking photographs or a videotape to document such demonstrations so you can share them later with students, parents, and administrators, and of course use for more summative purposes.

At times a product or an artifact is the result of a cycle of inquiry, for example: An array of liquids tested with red cabbage juice show which liquids are more basic and which are more acidic. Another product may be a poster showing the process the student(s) used, some results of earlier tests, charts or graphs of their results, and a summary of what they learned. Explaining this documentation requires students to reflect on what they learned and to communicate it to others, and enables you to check for overall understanding, ideas, and skills developed during investigations. It is important that students understand that such a product is not just a creative expression, but a demonstration of what they learned from their investigations. To make this clear, consider brainstorming with students the criteria for an effective product or presentation. Help them understand what it means to show what they learned, either by sharing products other students have created in the past, or by giving some examples. For instance, if fourth-grade students have been investigating the properties of light, one project criterion might be that they need to somehow show their understanding of straight-line motion and reflection. Once criteria have been established, you can refer to them as students create their products to help keep them focused on the elements they need to include. You and the students will then use the criteria to critique the products and presentations as they are shared with the class.

Culminating artifacts and products can take many forms. Consider the following suggestions for helping students summarize and/or express in various ways what they learned as a result of their investigations:

• Ask investigative groups to develop class presentations or dramatizations (e.g., how molecules move differently in solids, liquids, and gases) that describe a scientific discovery. Consider encouraging computer presentations (e.g., using HyperStudio software) that include photos, video clips, sound, and/or writing to explain an investigation.

• Ask students to help you create a display to "tell the story" of an investigation; it can include photos, student work, quotes, and/or excerpts of videotape or of audio transcripts. Ask students to help you select prints/clips/quotes to illustrate their investigative processes or new learnings.

• Have students write a piece titled, "What a Good Scientific Investigation Looks Like" or draw an image of a scientist, then discuss the thinking revealed by their work.

Other projects require students to apply what they've learned to a new situation, or to use their learning in a new way. Such projects challenge students to examine in a different way what they learned, and to determine what meaning it has for them. As students share and/or discuss such projects, their classmates also gain insights.

- Ask students to create demonstrations of scientific phenomena, based on an investigation, that other students can learn from, discuss, or emulate. For example, students can create liquid layers in a clear straw that show how liquids of different densities layer out when poured into a transparent container. Before pouring the liquids, presenters can ask the class to predict the order in which they think the layers will settle and why.

- Once they feel comfortable with a concept, ask students to create a series of investigative stations that would help younger children begin to understand the same concept. Pair up with a younger class and try out the ideas. Schedule a few exploration sessions with time in between for students to discuss challenges and successes and to revise their stations.

- Have students create a product at home or in school that challenges them to apply what they've learned about a concept; for example, after students discover the crayfish preference for dark over light, challenge them to create a simple shelter to add to the small swimming pool habitat the crayfish are kept in at school.

- Have students use the knowledge they gained during an investigation to create a "how-to" manual for carrying out an investigation. Have them use their manuals to teach students in another class about the phenomena/processes.

It is trial and error and practice over time that helps you embed these techniques and tools into your daily routine. There is a wealth of information for assessment of learning that students provide on a day-to-day basis. When you become aware of this opportunity for both facilitating and assessing learning, there are all kinds of positive outcomes for students and for your own teaching skills.

Once again, the NSES have summarized the practices teachers use in both facilitating and assessing student learning. In reading through the recommended techniques, you will see the statements "less emphasis . . . " and "more emphasis . . ." For instance, the Standards call for less emphasis on having teachers ask for recitation of acquired knowledge and more emphasis on providing opportunities for scientific discussion and debate among students (sparking science discussions); and less emphasis on "testing students for factual information at the end of the unit or chapter," shifting to more emphasis on "continuously assessing student understanding" (see Resource B, Table B.3, "NSES: Changing Emphases for Teaching").

Analyzing and Using Continuous Assessment Data

4

An important consideration when conducting continuous assessment is what you will do with the data as or after you collect it. Just as students analyze and use the information gathered during a science investigation, so too do you analyze the data and use the findings to inform instruction, promote student learning, and enhance your own professional growth. These are the primary benefits of this type of formative assessment. You can also gain an important secondary benefit in that you can use this assessment data for more summative purposes, such as reporting student progress to students, parents, and other teachers. In this chapter we look at the next steps to take as or after the data are collected; that is, the analysis and use of continuous assessment data.

ANALYSIS AND USE OF
CONTINUOUS ASSESSMENT DATA

When preparing for analysis and use of continuous assessment data, you need a clear vision of what you want to see in your students' science development. We asked in Chapter 2, "*What should we be collecting evidence of?*" In this chapter we ask, "*What should we be analyzing the data for?*" What are the concepts, processes, and habits of mind that you want the students to learn? What do they look like when they are demonstrated by students at their appropriate developmental level? You want to have these goals in mind not only when you facilitate the learning, and collect the evidence of learning, but also when you're ready to analyze the data for the purposes of assessment.

Just as the resources, NSES, Benchmarks, and your state and district frameworks are useful for planning and collecting data, the same resources are needed as we analyze the data. Table 4.1 provides a skeleton list for reference.

Table 4.1   Processes, Content Categories, & Scientific Habits of Mind

The Processes of Science	Science Content Categories	Scientific Habits of Mind
Questioning	Unifying Concepts and Processes	Honesty
Observing	Science as Inquiry	Curiosity
Planning and investigating	Physical Science	Perseverance
	Life Science	Balance of open mindedness with skepticism
Using scientific tools	Earth and Space Science	
Explaining, predicting, analyzing and interpreting data	Science and Technology	Reliance on evidence and a willingness to modify ideas
Communicating	Science in Personal and Social Perspectives	Clear and accurate expression and elaboration of ideas and alternative positions
	History and Nature of Science	

You may not be as familiar with the term *habits of mind* as you are with the processes and concepts of science. When we refer to the habits of mind we are talking about the dispositions, the values and attitudes scientists display as they do their work. While not defined as a separate body of standards in the NSES, habits of mind are described in the "Science as Inquiry" category of content standards and throughout the National Science Education Standards. The habits of mind are also described in Chapter 12 of *Benchmarks for Science Literacy* (American Association for the Advancement of Science, 1993).

Indicators of these standards are what you will look for as you analyze the data you collect. The more you use standards, the more you will become clear about what they are and what to look for as evidence of your students' learning.

Analysis of Data Promotes Equity in Practice

Do you frequently visit one group of children more than others while they are investigating? Which children do you have a lot of information on? A little information about? How do the number of interactions you have with girls compare with those that you make with boys? You will find the answers to these questions and others in the student data you collect. Being clear about the standards you want your students to achieve and maintaining good records helps you see what and whom you have been focusing on to date. Gaps in your records show which standards and which students you need to pay more attention to. Having a working knowledge of the standards helps you determine the concepts and skills you need to get to for the first time or to reinforce, and what you haven't yet addressed. Looking over your records, you are more able to see the information you may be missing on individual students. Being clear on the learning goals and having good records that show who you need data for also helps remind you about how well you are paying attention to special-needs students and gender issues. By having a composite record of all of your students, you will be able to be equitable in your practices toward all students.

HOW DO YOU ANALYZE CONTINUOUS ASSESSMENT DATA?

"Analyze vt... 1: to separate into parts for study." The word *analyze* may conjure up columns of data, calculators, figures, and so forth. When you think about analysis of data, you are reminded that you planned for inquiry with certain learning goals in mind, and, therefore, you will use these same goals to analyze your documentation. When your students are in the midst of their inquiries, you encourage them to make sense of their data and communicate their findings. The same is true when you analyze the data you've collected from students as they are engaged in investigations. It is matching the evidence you document to the goals you've set that allows you to see where the students are, what they have accomplished, and what they still need to do. Gradually you will get used to sorting and to matching the evidence you collect to the goals you've set while you are with the students or at a later time. As you listen in on conversations students are having with one another, or review a tape or photographs or your notes, you may find it helpful to ask yourself questions like the following:

"What is it I am finding in these data?"

"What do they tell me about this child or this small group of students?"

"In what ways do the data match the original concept, process, and disposition goals I set at the beginning of the unit?"

"How can I use this information to plan tomorrow's class?"

"What can I do in the next several days to respond to what I'm learning about my students' development in science?"

"What can I do in future units to promote or eliminate certain aspects of the lesson?"

"What key evidence do I want to save?"

An important reminder is that the analysis of a situation can happen on the spot or the data can be quickly analyzed after class or after school. The findings you make will be of great help to you when you use them to make instructional decisions, monitor growth in all children, enhance students' understanding, and reflect on your own teaching practices. These findings are also useful when reporting student progress in a summative way.

Throughout the rest of the chapter you will find examples of how to make effective use of the data you've collected using the tools and techniques you learned about in the previous chapter.

HOW DO YOU USE CONTINUOUS ASSESSMENT DATA?

Using Continuous Assessment Data to Make Decisions

Decision making is a primary use of continuous assessment (CA) data. Sometimes the decision is made while you are working with students and/or upon reflecting on a situation. One situation that requires you to make instructional decisions quickly is when students' investigations produce unexpected results. When this occurs, you are faced with the decision to continue with your plans or to pause and reflect with students on the investigations. This happened to a fourth-grade teacher in the context of a unit on nutrition.

In order to compare the amount of sugar in various foods, students needed to learn first how to test for the presence of sugar. To observe how yeast works as an indicator for sugar, students were given two plastic "baggies"—one filled part way with flour, the other part way with sugar. Students were instructed to add a measure of yeast and a measure of warm water to each baggie, then to seal them, put them in a warm water bath, and notice what happened. The expected result was that in the sugar baggie, the yeast would dissolve in the warm water and be kept warm by the water bath, and would react with the sugar and create carbon dioxide, which would then inflate the bag. The baggie with flour would not inflate (because it had no sugar for the yeast to live on). In this case not much happened in either bag. The teacher guessed that either the water hadn't been warm enough, or that the yeast had been too old to react with the sugar.

The teacher found herself at the point of needing to make a decision. On her mind were the plans she had made for next day's investigation. The test they were going to do assumed the students had knowledge of how yeast could work as an indicator for the presence of sugar in cereal. The plan was for the students to mix yeast, water, and one type of cereal as a way to determine and compare amounts of sugar in a variety of cereals. The more sugar in the cereal, the more food the yeast would have to live and grow, the more carbon dioxide the yeast would give off, and the more the baggie would swell up. Feeling pressure to get to the next day's lesson, the teacher really wanted to tell students what was supposed to have happened in today's lesson in order to be ready for tomorrow's lesson. She refrained from doing this, and decided they would revisit the

Figure 4.1   One ziplock bag with flour, and yeast with water from a measuring cup

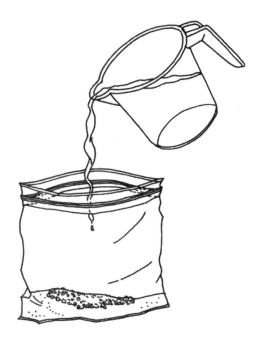

investigation. She knew in making this decision she was not going to be able to "get through" the whole kit because she could keep the kit for only a certain number of weeks before she had to send it on to the next teacher. This consideration weighed on her mind, but when she considered the real goals of doing science, she knew the students would have to experience the test in order to apply it to another situation. She had some ideas why the results of the test hadn't worked as anticipated and saw this as an opportunity for the students to have the experience of dealing with variables.

The teacher remembered in her earlier discussion with the students that almost all of them had experience with yeast, and how it bubbled up when put in warm water. She decided to ask the students again about optimal living conditions for yeast, and in doing this the students came up with three reasons why the yeast did not react. They decided that the temperature of the water would matter; water that was too hot could have killed the yeast, whereas water that was too cool could inhibit any growth at all. They also offered the idea that there is a date on the yeast package and perhaps the yeast that was in the kit might be too old.

Together they planned the next day's investigation. They would test three types of yeast: outdated yeast (the teacher knew she had several packets in her refrigerator), a new package from the grocery store, and a third set-up with the

Figure 4.2   Two ziplock bags with yeast, flour or sugar, and water in a water bath

yeast in the kit. One group put the yeast in separate baggies with a little sugar in each, and then added lukewarm water as the directions on the packet called for. Another group would set up the same test with the combination of yeast and flour in baggies. Another group thought it would be good to test a new package of yeast and sugar in cold water and compare it with the same set-up with lukewarm water. And the fourth group wanted to test a new package of yeast and sugar in water hot enough for tea and compare it with the same set-up with lukewarm water.

All of this planning and figuring out of the variables took some time, but the students and the teacher knew that by the end of the next day, they would have some good information about how this system works and how yeast can be used as an indicator.

The teacher decided that the potential gain in taking this "side trip" away from the curriculum would outweigh the experience of following the curriculum day by day. Knowing that the students would be clear in their conceptual understanding of the growth of yeast as an indicator for sugar would affect how she set up other experiences in the unit that built on this one. Her decision also meant that her students would have an opportunity to practice important science processes and dispositions: identifying variables, being honest about data, being curious about investigation results, analyzing and interpreting results critically, persevering with investigations that don't go as planned, and so on.

These kinds of decisions can be difficult for a teacher to make. Time is a constant challenge in the classroom, and teachers less experienced with inquiry may be uncomfortable straying from their plans or from the flow of the curriculum. On the other hand, the gains that can come from addressing unexpected results with students are great—for you in what you can learn about students, and for students in conceptual understanding and practice of science processes and dispositions.

Using Data to Serve Instruction While Monitoring Growth

You will find you are able to describe changes in your students' understanding and skills by observing them closely and monitoring changes over time. Using continuous assessment techniques and tools helps you capture what students are doing and thinking, with or without your intervention. Using what you see and hear on a day-to-day basis helps you to make informed instructional decisions and to plan your next steps to move students forward in their growth. Also, the information can be part of a feedback loop for the students that can help them recognize where they are in the investigation and what to do next. The action you take based on the data to support your students' growth can be immediate, the next day, or over the long term of the unit or of the year.

> *"I believe that my primary job as teacher is to look at students' strengths and decide next steps to help them move further."*

Third- and Fourth-Grade Teacher

Take a look into a Kindergarten classroom to see the students engaged in an inquiry using "ice balloons" and see the kinds of decisions the teacher made based on in the data she collected. See http://www.exploratorium.edu/ifi/activities/iceballoons/iceballoons.html as a source for the ice balloons unit.

While working with her Kindergarten class in a unit on changes in states of matter and the role of temperature in this process, Mrs. F introduced the students to ice balloons (balloons that have been filled with water and then put in the freezer for a few days before using them in class). In talking with Megan, she realized that Megan had a great idea about putting the ice balloon in the sunlight to see the effect it had on melting the ice. Mrs. F immediately said, "Megan, I'm going to write down that idea!" They discussed how the sunlight might affect the balloon differently than the room light. Knowing that an object will increase in temperature with increased radiation, Mrs. F knew Megan's

Figure 4.3   Ice balloon on a tray

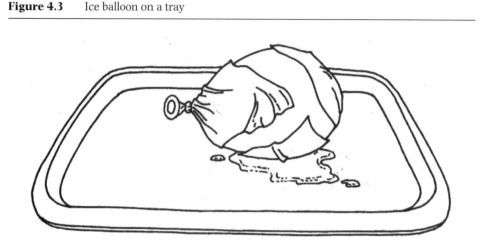

idea would make a good investigation for the whole class to witness. She wanted to provide Megan and the other students with an opportunity to begin to understand the role that heat plays in the changing states of matter. She knew from experience that children at the Kindergarten level can understand the notion of greater and lesser amounts of heat and how this affects the melting of the ice. On the spot, Mrs. F made the decision to share Megan's idea with the rest of the class. She wanted Megan and the other students to think more deeply about the differences between these two sources of heat in relation to their effect on melting an ice balloon and see how they might go about planning an investigation to test this idea.

Using Data to Enhance
Student Learning: Deeper Learning

In the process of monitoring student growth and planning next steps based on what you observe your students saying and doing, you will find yourself thinking of new ideas for how to enhance student learning and take under-standing to a deeper level. You know well that focusing only on getting the "right" results in an investigation or on memorizing vocabulary will not pro-mote deep understanding of the concept. As teachers help students reflect on their ideas and investigative processes, greater understanding and skill levels emerge, and new ideas for investigation and discussion come up. You can use this opportunity to spark deeper student thinking and growth.

Mrs. F knows that students of this age and stage of development have difficulty articulating their own questions for investigation. They can "try out" things, in this case, on their ice balloons, but don't often express a question orally before trying it out. For example, they might sprinkle salt on a patch of the ice balloon before articulating a question such as, "I wonder what will happen if I sprinkle salt on my ice balloon?" or before making a prediction.

So, when she brought forth Megan's idea in a scientists' meeting at the end of the first day, Mrs. F wanted to find out what ideas and questions the students might have about possible sources of heat and how heat figures into the concept of changes in the state of matter. She also wanted to listen to their ideas about how to plan and carry out an investigation to test their ideas, and what they predicted would happen. Mrs. F also wanted to reinforce the idea that they, the students, can find out things for themselves by their own actions, just as scientists do.

The students had lots of ideas about sources of heat for melting the ice— next to the heater, on top of a stove. They all agreed that sunlight was a good possibility as a source for heat, because they had all experienced sitting by the classroom window when the sun came in during the afternoon. One student offered a prediction that the sunlight would make the ice melt faster. Mrs. F asked them, "Faster than what?" From the students' ideas of how fast an ice balloon would melt, she helped the students articulate a comparison question involving the two different sources of light as that related to heat over a certain period of time. One source was the window and the afternoon sunlight, and another source, the overhead classroom lights.

The next afternoon as the students were observing the ice balloons, one left in the sunlight, the other out of the direct sunlight, other questions began to surface. It started with one student wondering about how the size and shape of the ice balloons might affect the melting. Mrs. F was excited to hear these ideas because they provided a segue to the notion of variables. She knew she could introduce variables in a very simple way by asking the questions with phrases such as, "Does it matter if . . .": "Does it matter if the balloons are the same size to begin with?" "Does it matter if the balloons are the same shape?" ". . . if the balloons are made out of water or apple juice?" "Which would melt first?" was another comparison question they used.

Throughout the investigation, Mrs. F was able to build their current understanding of sources of heat as well as the role heat played in the changes in states of matter to a much deeper level. She also was able to lay the foundation for the concept of variables and fair testing. Conversations led to many other ideas for investigations. Again, when appropriate, Mrs. F helped the students to articulate their ideas as comparison questions.

One student wanted to put an ice balloon in a place where there was no light. Upon probing, Mrs. F recognized that this student was making a connection between light and heat. This student's idea led to setting up another investigation with an ice balloon in the light and another in the dark. Going deeper with the idea of sources of heat, some students investigated other sources of heat to see how quickly an ice cube could melt. Another idea surfaced about how to keep an ice balloon (or ice cube) from melting. This idea provided a segue to her introducing a concept related to sources of heat and changes in the states of matter, that of "insulation" and how it might affect the change from ice to water.

The ice balloon lesson could have been just an activity that was good for improving observational skills. Mrs. F could have focused on the observation aspect of ice changing state by melting into water when she collected assessment data. Instead this experience turned out to be an investigation that led to conceptual understanding, identification of variables, critical thinking, and the skills of observation and measurement. When Megan happened on an idea for investigating the role heat had in changing the solid into liquid, she opened the door for further exploration of heat sources, comparative melting rates, and variables such as size and shape. A question starter such as, "Does it make a difference if . . ." helped with the design of other comparative investigations. Other important learnings were reinforced throughout the investigation, including practice in the processes of questioning, planning and carrying out investigations, and the disposition that they, as scientists, could find out answers about their world, just as scientists do.

> *"Using the Inquiry/CA approach, students communicate on a more ongoing basis with their immediate peers, and so they get ideas from each other as to what they tried and what happened. At the end of the day, they go back and rethink and retry ideas with the materials far more often than they had previously. Now it's not so much the teacher telling the students, for example, this is what density means. They get to hear it from many other sources and have a chance to mull over their ideas and go back to their journals and re-look at a picture from three weeks ago and take a fresh look at something. And the result is conceptual change in students' ideas about a science phenomenon."*
>
> —Sixth-Grade Teacher

Using Continuous Assessment Data to Support Students' Conceptual Growth

It would be very easy for me to lecture to a class about how we displaced a certain amount of liquid, and just go on about it. But then down the line I'd find out that they had no concept of what I meant by the 'displaced liquid.' Suppose that instead of just listening to me, my students actually collected that displaced liquid for themselves. Then when we are talking about the Archimedes principle, we all know what we are talking about as opposed to if we hadn't had that experience with real fluid undergoing a real displacement. (Bob Prigo, in *The Essence of Continuous Assessment*, Center for Continuous Education, 2001)

Another context in which it is very helpful to use continuous assessment to inform your instruction is tracking students' emergent conceptual understanding. You can observe and elicit students' understanding by asking questions, watching how children interact with materials, listening to their conversations, reading their journals, and so on. This paying attention to students' understanding becomes continuous assessment when you do it *throughout investigations*, rather than just at the end, and when you use the information you gain to adapt your teaching. This is a critical piece in helping students to grow in their understanding of science concepts. If you wait until the end of the unit to assess what students understand, you may miss out on numerous "teachable moments," which may then result in students not getting as far in that understanding as they might have. For example, a very skilled third-fourth teacher provided her students with a variety of experiences over several weeks to help them understand concepts around electricity. These activities included class discussions, some direct teaching, and lots of hands-on time with batteries, bulbs, and switches. To wrap up the unit and get a sense of students' conceptual growth, she asked them to develop a final project that would demonstrate what they had learned about electricity. She was fairly confident that the majority of students understood how series and parallel circuits worked, how switches worked, and the effects of resistance. When their projects were completed, students explained them to small groups of visiting students, teachers, and parents rotating around the room. In order to capture students' explanations, the teacher asked a professional developer she was working with on inquiry to interview students on videotape about their projects and what they had learned.

The teacher learned a great deal from watching the videotape. In general, she was surprised to discover that many students had a more tentative grasp of the concepts than she had thought. She was particularly surprised to find that one group seemed not to understand electrical resistance (the fact that a conductor can offer resistance to the flow of the charge). She decided to show the whole class a section of the video on which the professional developer had questioned that group. As she and the class watched the clip, the teacher discovered that the majority of students were unclear about this concept.

While the teacher was discouraged to discover this, she was delighted to find that watching and discussing the videotape sparked students' curiosity about resistance and offered her a "teachable moment." Though she felt she didn't have much time left in her schedule for the unit, she and the students did do some additional investigating. They tested some very long, very thin copper wire and compared it to the regular gauge copper wire from their electricity kit. They found with the thin wire that the length of the wire did make a difference in completing a circuit and making a bulb light. As a result of this brief reteaching session, the teacher felt that most of the students significantly strengthened their understanding of resistance.

Through these experiences, this teacher learned a great deal about the power of using videotape as a continuous assessment tool. She realized how much she could learn about her students' conceptual understanding by watching the tape herself, and how she could spark discussion and opportunities for deeper learning by showing the tape to her students. She also learned the importance of engaging in continuous assessment throughout a unit and decided, in the future, she would use the videotaping tool earlier in the unit rather than just at the end.

Using Data to Reflect on Your Teaching

One of the most powerful outcomes of using continuous assessment is finding what happens to your own practice as a result of observing and listening to your students and reflecting on their growth. You will find you are also looking at your own teaching as well. You will find yourself becoming more purposeful about the techniques and tools you use. You may also find that it helps to get together with another teacher or a small group of teachers to talk about what is happening in your class. In a way it's a form of professional development you provide for yourself. The following quotes represent changes teachers are making as a result of reflecting on their own practice.

*"I began to bring thoughts into focus by reflecting upon my own teaching style. Because questioning can either promote or stifle discussion, I have been working on asking 'productive' questions and allowing students 'think time' before answering. I am asking more 'What would happen if . . .?' type of questions. Instead of just asking a 'why?' question, I am trying to ask 'why do **you** think that . . .?' questions that will elicit the*

students' thinking process. The 'why?' questions can intimidate the students and they become more hesitant to share answers/ideas that they fear may be 'wrong.'"

—Fifth- and Sixth-Grade Teacher

"Before, I wasn't as interested in what they were thinking but I had a vision of where they needed to go. I may have a little mini lecture here or there to make sure they get those key words or facts and have them in their journal. Now I've found a way to fit the concepts in to our conversations. I'm much more inquisitive about their inquisitiveness."

—Third- and Fourth-Grade Teacher

Chapter 6 focuses on the professional development aspect of reflecting on the data you are collecting. In this chapter, in the sections "Continuous Assessment as Professional Development" and "Reflecting, Analyzing, and Learning With Colleagues" you will find suggestions for ways to analyze assessment data, and to work with colleagues to forward your own professional growth.

Using Continuous Assessment Data to Report on Students' Progress

By listening to and closely observing your students' talking, carrying out investigations, sharing ideas, and showing their results, you can accumulate a wealth of information that can be used formatively for feedback to your students, as well as summative for reports. Making sense of the data for reporting purposes should link back to your learning goals. Once again, for accuracy and congruity, it is best if your goals for desired learning outcomes align with the student learning experiences you facilitate and assess, and also with what you report on in terms of student progress. Data from ongoing assessments provide an accurate picture of students' growth in science and how their understanding, abilities, and dispositions change over time. The challenge for you lies in having the data accessible to you in a way that will provide an accurate summary of students' understanding of science concepts and their abilities to think and work like scientists. You want to be able to provide this information for the students themselves, for their parents, and for other teachers.

There are many ways to report student and program growth. Growth in science does not have to be confined to a quarterly report card. You can use and benefit from a range of informal reporting opportunities throughout the year to showcase your science programs and the students' progress.

Informal Reporting:
Information About the Student

Panels and Emergent Bulletin Boards. Teachers make visual displays/panels or emergent bulletin boards to get the material up quickly so that it can affect what's happening in the classroom. These displays serve as feedback to the students, who discuss them with the teacher and each other and in the process generate new ideas to test and take their learning deeper.

Parent Conferences. Parent conferences are settings where teachers can tell parents what they are finding out about their children. By using continuous assessment data, teachers have notes, photographs, and artifacts to back up the statements they make about a student.

Newsletters. Send home a "What's happening this week in science" section in your newsletter to parents, rather than just an announcement such as, "This week, the third grade studied amphibians." Try vignettes about the questions students raised about tadpoles and frogs and what they did to find answers and new information by doing investigations.

Informal Reporting:
Information About the Science Program

"Science Bags." These are a form of informal reporting of both student and programmatic information. When a teacher sends home materials or a home assignment that engages the family in the science of their child's classroom, the parents see how well their student is doing science and what the science program focuses on. One version of "science bags" contains simple materials and an activity card, and a comment sheet that the child and her family can try out at home. The activity card is always written in an open-ended fashion. In some cases, there is a literature book, a comment sheet, along with a related science activity that the family can read and do. The comment sheet allows parents to describe not only what they did and found out during the investigation, but also any opinions about what their child is doing and learning in science.

Science Nights. Science Nights are another popular way to bring alive your science program for parents. When parents and students come to school at night to "do" science together, parents can experience for themselves the type of science their children are doing and what they're learning. As they talk in groups about the results of their investigation, you can model continuous assessment techniques and tools.

Parent and Administrator Visits. Inviting important people to your classroom is a way to disseminate a view of inquiry-based science and continuous assessment.

> *"One of my endeavors was to create a visual display, which I refer to as a 'panel,' to inform students, colleagues, administrators, and parents about the investigations going on in my kindergarten classroom. I used a video printer to produce pictures of the children at work, choosing six significant frames. I copied and enlarged the prints, then affixed transcriptions of the students' actual language below each print. I learned that it was important to include my interpretation of a child's exploration with the transcription on a large piece. All of this was mounted on large pieces of oak tag with a title and appropriate headings. My additions enabled readers to understand how the child's cycle of inquiry—raising questions, trying out ideas, arriving at a solution, and communicating results—was represented in a kindergartner's investigation.*
>
> *"I wondered how I could use this same process of visual panels to document learning over a period of time. Instead of making display panels after the fact, it made sense to get the material up quickly so it would affect what's happening in the classroom. I wanted to use panels to give children information about what's happening in the classroom, so we could discuss what's posted and it could get children to think about investigation in other ways. As children test new ideas and modify their explorations, additional evidence of their thinking is posted."*
>
> —Pat Fitzsimmons

Formal Reporting. The reporting-out piece is a snapshot of where a student is at that particular place in the time, based on all the pieces of information gathered.

> *"When I plan to report out (write report cards), I sit with my raw notes, refer back to the 'IT' [see Chapter 2, Inquiry/Standards-Based Science: What Does It Look Like?], and write a narrative to fit our standards-based report card. For the report card, I have to provide a score between one and four in three categories for science: Investigative Ability, Content, Communicate Results. The score, of course, only gives a rough gauge of where kids are at a point in time. In addition, I also always do a narrative about students' strengths and areas to work on in each area based on my rough observation notes."*
>
> —Fourth-Grade Teacher

The Report Card. In many cases the format required for reporting is a school-based decision and may take the form of a narrative, of grades only, of report cards with categories using standards-based language, and so on. Some report cards limit while others encourage description of student gains and needs. Reporting is also a way for you to reinforce for your students and their parents the goals of learning you have for your students. The language of the standards and summaries, such as *Inquiry/Standards-Based Science: What Does It Look Like?* (Chapter 2, Figure 2.2) helps to provide that accurate picture.

Ideally, the report describes what a child is doing/able to do and will be doing in the future in the areas of conceptual development, and the child's abilities to think and work like a scientist. A reporting system may encourage or limit the valuable information you can collect using continuous assessment.

When a child brings home a report card with the following information, what does it tell the student and the parent?

Science: Mary Smith

Qualities	1st quarter	2nd quarter	3rd quarter	4th quarter
WORKS WELL IN GROUPS	NI	P	PF	
PARTICIPATES IN CLASS	P	P	PF	
WORK IS NEAT	NI	P	P	

NI = needs improvement; P = progressing; PF = proficient

A poor-quality reporting system can limit teachers who practice continuous assessment. Because these teachers have in mind what good science looks like, they may collect data that goes well beyond what the reporting system calls for. If they are limited by the form the report card takes, teachers may be discouraged from continuing to collect this valuable information.

A report card that places less value on science than on other subjects may include one or two phrases such as: LIKES SCIENCE or CAN WORK IN A GROUP, but not allow for information on a child's growth in science understanding, abilities, or dispositions.

Compare the "**Science**: Mary Smith" report card (above) with one that provides authentic information about the child's growth in conceptual understanding, and the processes, skills, and dispositions of science.

Mary's progress in Science

Unit Study: For the past 4 weeks we have been studying Fluids, focusing on the concepts of density, buoyancy, and pressure, the processes of raising questions and devising investigations, and the dispositions of being curious and desiring knowledge.

Conceptual Development: Mary is beginning to understand the concept of density as it relates to buoyancy and pressure. She has explored solids and their ability to float, liquids and the way they layer on each other, and gases in terms of warm or "lighter" air by making a hot air balloon.

The Processes of Science (process skills): Mary is able to move forward when given a question to test and is beginning to raise her own questions although they are not always "testable." Next we will work on expressing them in a testable form. She has also moved beyond one-step planning and is beginning to plan a "fair" test. Next we will work on using variables in her tests and planning all the steps of the investigation.

The Learning Habits (dispositions of science): Because of Mary's attention to raising her own questions and beginning to plan "fair" tests, she is demonstrating more curiosity as she really becomes invested in her "I wonder what will happen if . . .?" or "Does it matter if . . .?" questions. She is beginning to seek knowledge for herself. As she becomes more able to plan investigations with variables we will work on relying on data, and being skeptical of data that don't seem to follow the patterns of our other observations.

In this progress report, the goals are clearly defined and Mary's progress is reported as a point on a continuum of development. Not only are the parents and student told where she is in terms of growth, but also what the next steps are for promoting Mary's growth.

Next we'll look at continuous assessment in the context of science inquiry as you read a story of Ms R, a third-grade teacher, as she plans for, facilitates, and assesses a unit on Light. Note the way she collects information and uses the data to make decisions, to take learning deeper, to reflect on her own practice, and to report her students' progress.

Vignette
Exploring Light

The following vignette provides one teacher's view as she plans a unit on light, facilitates opportunities for inquiry, uses continuous assessment techniques and tools to gather data, and analyzes the evidence of her goals. She uses the findings for both formative and summative purposes. That is, she uses the findings for reflecting on her students' understanding, for reflecting on her own teaching, and for recording the data for future reporting.

Ms. R was planning a unit on light for her Grade 3 elementary classroom. Her goal was to have the students begin to understand some basic concepts of light by conducting investigations with simple light-related materials and then making sense of their findings. She hoped that by exploring light through student investigations, she would be helping her students to set a firm foundation for emerging concepts such as: *light travels in a straight line*, and *light can be reflected, refracted (bent), dispersed (broken into its component parts), and absorbed.* She also planned on working with her students to *identify sources of light.* In addition to developing these concepts, she wanted the students to practice and improve their use of the processes of science of *making accurate observations, using scientific tools, predicting*, and *communicating processes and findings;* and *the* dispositions of science of *curiosity, perseverance*, and a *willingness to modify ideas based on evidence.*

Along with thinking about the investigations and gathering the materials, Ms. R planned the various ways she would collect information about students' progress while they were engaged in their explorations.

On the first day of the unit, Ms. R offered students an "invitation to learn" by asking them what they could find out about light by using a flashlight and a mirror. She gave one flashlight and two flat mirrors to each student pair and watched as they eagerly accepted the materials and went to work. While they worked, Ms. R visited with the groups and *took notes* about what the students were doing with the materials. Students called her over many times to talk about what they were doing and finding out. In response to her query, *"Tell me what you are finding out,"* Ms. R was able to record a few responses from almost every group.

After school, Ms. R met with her partner teacher to debrief what happened during class. She and the other second-grade teacher had decided to plan and begin the light unit together. Ms. R had some expectations that the children might use the hand-held mirrors and the flashlights to explore the reflections of light. Instead, she told her friend, *"Many of the students chose to 'build' with the materials. Kids piled a mirror or mirrors on top of the flashlight and turned the switch on and off; or they put the mirror flat on the rug and set the lit flashlight facing down on top of the mirror. Even when I tried to suggest distancing the flashlight from the mirror or angling the beam of light toward the mirror, the students continued to arrange the materials as if they needed to be in close contact with each other."*

Ms. R discussed many things about the class with her partner teacher. They discussed how young students seem to need to get used to the materials by playing with them. They also discussed that perhaps by using both a mirror and a flashlight there may have been too much stimulus in their first exploration. Her partner teacher suggested that Ms. R may have had a particular finding in mind that she wanted the students to notice, and this might have influenced how she perceived the lesson. Her partner confessed that she often found herself directing the children to do a specific exploration. She gave Ms. R an example of what she meant: *"I suggested a few things like take your mirrors and stand opposite each other. I told them to move back and forth but look into each other's mirror. I urged them to tell each other what they were seeing."* The two teachers discussed the benefits and drawbacks of prompting student investigation. They chuckled at the honest conversation they were having and how it felt good to be working together on the science unit.

> Continuous assessment enables a teacher's own professional growth. Ms. R used her observations and documentation and conversation with her partner teacher to reflect on her teaching. The partners supported each other by personalizing the professional development through planning, implementing, and talking about students and practice.

That night, as she thought about the class and her discussion with her teacher partner, Ms. R decided that it would be interesting to find out what the students learned on their own as they explored. She also decided that she would give the students only flashlights to use the next day. When she saw her partner and mentioned her idea, her partner said, *"I think I'll use only mirrors today. It will be fun to compare notes on how the students respond to these changes!"*

> Continuous assessment serves instruction and decision making. Here Ms. R used her data and her conversation with her partner teacher to serve instruction by making decisions about the next best steps for her class and their early study of light. Her partner piggy-backed this idea but changed it to suit her own interests.

The next day the students explored with flashlights for about fifteen minutes. While they were investigating, Ms. R made notes on a clipboard of things the students were trying *(teacher observation notes)*. She also noted questions students were asking each other, like, *"I wonder what it looks like if we shine the flashlight along the wall? How far can we back up and still have it show on the wall?"* *"What would happen if we covered half of the flashlight with a piece of black paper? Could we make it look like a laser beam?"*

At the end of the class, she told her students they would be having a scientists' meeting *(sparking student conversations)*. She asked them to take a few minutes to draw a picture and write as best they could about what they found out that day *(student science notebooks)*.

In the group circle of student scientists, she asked them to share what they did and what they found out, and probed them for clear explanations of their findings. Ms. R enjoyed the many interesting points that her students reported. The student explorations were typical of that age group, including: shining the flashlight on the wall, making finger puppets in front of the flashlight so that they would show up on the wall, placing the flashlight under their shirts and shining the light outward through their shirt, and two students crawled under a pile of pillows in the reading center to see what the light looked like in a "really dark place." They said they got the idea from the times they had put a flashlight under the bed covers at home. Some students put the flashlight behind the window curtain and discovered that some light passed through; others built a "house" in the block center and set it up so that the light from the flashlight shown through one of the windows. They looked in each other's mouths and reported that the light made their mouths bright and the light helped them see details of their mouths.

Ms. R also shared with the students some of the things she had written on her clipboard as she traveled around the room *listening closely* to what the children were discussing. While the students were explaining their discoveries, she jotted down a list of their observations on a large piece of chart paper with students' names next to their offerings for all to see. She often probed what the students thought about what they noticed ("*Tell us more about that. What do you think was going on?*") and what they would like to try next *(purposeful questioning)*. Sometimes she added a question that a student asked to the *chart paper documentation*.

She realized that she was featuring and assessing the process skill of communication in multiple ways—through students' talking, drawing, writing, and then reporting to the class.

Continuous assessment serves instruction while monitoring growth. In this case, Ms. R used a variety of techniques to collect information; for example, the use of student science notebooks, as well as the use of chart paper jottings, not only helped her to facilitate instruction, but it also gave her some artifacts to help determine where the students were with their ideas.

Continuous assessment provides information for reporting student progress.

Ms. R urged her students to use their science notebooks so they would have a log of their thinking as they started the unit that they could refer back to in order to see how their observations and explanations changed or stayed the same throughout the unit. Later she and the student could look back on these examples to help determine student growth in ideas, or process skills, or habits of mind. She was also able to listen to the children's short presentations describing their findings and to record on a large piece of chart paper a few notes next to the names of the presenters. It helped her to realize that formative assessment does not begin and end with the investigation periods. There was much to learn of the inquiry/assessment process at these other important moments, such as *discussions* and *presentations*.

Near the end of the scientists' meeting, Ms. R felt that this was an appropriate time for her to weave into her discussion the idea of light sources (*sharing new information),* and so she asked the students to identify other sources of light besides their flashlights. The children were quick to identify light fixtures and lamps in their homes, camping lanterns, lightning bugs, stoplights, the sun, and automobile headlights. She encouraged the students to talk to their parents that night about light and to look for sources of light in their homes *(applying knowledge to a new learning situation)*.

Ms. R talked over the days' happenings with her partner teacher. Recently, they had been studying the importance of listening to students' ideas in their professional development workshops on constructivist teaching and learning. In this study they had come to realize, whether the children's ideas were scientifically correct or not, they were a jumping-off point for testing these ideas and building new understanding. The chart paper with the children's ideas next to their names would be useful documentation to reflect on as the unit progressed.

Another purpose the chart paper served was to show the teachers who hadn't yet had a chance to contribute to the conversation. In their interest to provide equal learning opportunities for all, the teacher partners decided they would start with these students in tomorrow's discussion.

> Continuous assessment enhances student learning while honoring existing student conceptions and everyday experiences.

Ms. R was able to extend her students' thinking and understanding as they reflected on their own experiences. Teachers familiar with constructivist approaches realize the importance of connecting new ideas to the ideas already held by the learner. Rather than beginning her unit on light with a question-and-answer session on, "Tell me what you already know about light," Ms. R chose to spend a couple of days on investigation. Now she is more prepared to seek all of the students' conceptions as they connect the new learning to home assignments and to what is happening every day in the classroom.

Over the course of the light unit the students tested out their own ideas and questions in addition to investigating specific activities that their teacher set up for them. They used "light boxes" from the school's box of light materials and placed the boxes on top of large sheets of white newsprint paper on the floor.

They placed objects in front of the beam of light to cast shadows on the white paper, traced the shadows of the objects onto the paper with markers, and then compared the tracings with the actual objects.

Ms. R took some digital pictures of the class while they were engaged in their investigations. Later she and a parent volunteer would talk to the students about what they were doing and finding out at the time the photo was taken. They also encouraged the students to write (or tell them what to write) about what was going on in the photo at that exact moment *(using photographs to reflect on student learning)*.

When the students were given a mirror to hold in front of the light beam, they traced the beam of light to the mirror and then out of the mirror at the angle the beam created. The white paper became their record sheets for that day. In fact, some of the students asked for a ruler in order to "get the line straight." As they reviewed their results on these record sheets, Ms. R asked them what they noticed. The students described what they found in each case, that the path of the light beam was a straight line. Some students noticed the line of light to the mirror and then out of the mirror as being like "a basketball off a backboard." In talking over this finding with her partner teacher, they decided it would be a good segue into an exploration of the idea of light entering and leaving a flat mirror. Ms. R and her partner made a note to arrange for a class time when all the students could explore this idea. She knew that it would be a good way to focus on the idea of light traveling in a straight line as well as to notice and ponder the light reflecting from the mirror—the angle "in" and the angle "out." She remembered the discussion she had had with her partner teacher after the first light lesson about "letting the children decide" versus "when the teacher decides to give suggestions." They commented that there is a time and a place for both types of facilitation.

Continuous assessment enhances student learning.

Ms. R was able to catalyze "deeper" thinking and understanding as the students reflected on their own experiences. As she planned for a more focused inquiry about light traveling in straight lines and the angles of reflection, she looked forward to the ideas of the learners that would result from the investigation.

Another time during this six-week unit on light, the students were given prisms to use. When they placed the prisms in front of the light box beam, they discovered that light could be separated. During another *scientists' meeting,* with Ms. R's guidance and the discussion among the group, they added these new learnings about light to their previous ideas.

Light travels in a straight line.

Light can be bent at an angle when it bounces off a reflective surface like a mirror or is directed through water.

Light can be separated into colors.

Ms. R set up more opportunities for the students to explore light and helped them use their new knowledge for explanations. The students made mazes with mirrors and blocks for the light to shine into and bounce off of. They challenged each other to construct a block maze with a couple of twists and turns. By careful positioning of mirrors, they felt the satisfaction of "structural engineers" as the light made its way into and out of their constructions. Students were challenged by Ms. R's question about shining a flashlight into a hole on the side of a shoebox so that it would come out another hole along the same side of the box. The flashlight was placed in front of one hole facing into the shoebox and onto a mirror fastened on the opposite side of the box. The trick was to angle the flashlight at the mirror and see the spot on the same wall that the bounced light reflected onto. This would be where the second hole should be cut.

Throughout the unit, Ms. R captured evidence of her students doing the processes of science and exhibiting the dispositions of scientists as well as making sense of their findings. At times she would *sit and listen closely* to a group and use a *clipboard to capture notes* about the students as they worked. Once she used *a tape recorder* and set it down next to a pair of students diligently working on their

Figure 4.4   Shoebox with mirror and flashlight

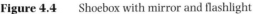

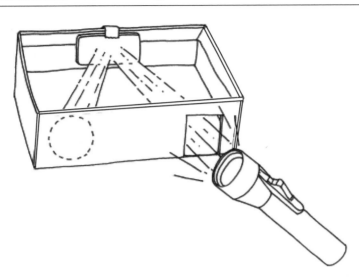

project. She listened to the tape on her drive home and found that one of the students was taking charge of all of the decisions related to the investigation. She used this information to suggest some changes to the girls on the next day. One of her bulletin boards was filled with digital photographs of the students doing science. Next to the photos were sentences written by the children explaining the main ideas. Like headlines in a newspaper, these sentence strips captured a great deal of information concerning the science development taking place among her students. All of these data will help her at report card time to describe how the students were progressing on their science goals during this unit.

Continuous assessment helps to monitor student growth.

Continuous assessment provides information to report student progress. Ms. R really looked forward to parent conferences so that she could tell parents what she was finding out about the youngsters. Now she could give specific examples to accompany and back up a statement such as, "He is working to improve in the area of explaining the results of his experiments. He's a persistent scientist, never tiring of trying endless variations within one of his light investigations. However, his comments, drawings, and writing do not tell the complete story of the discoveries that he has made. We're working to improve these communication skills."

At the end of the unit, Ms. R was thinking about how she would have the students apply their knowledge and take their learning in new directions. She suggested that the students do a "light" puppet show for their classmates.

Many issues came up as they were setting up for the show. One was dealing with where to put the audience. They realized that having the light source, the puppets, and the student puppeteers in front of the audience, between the audience and the screen, would cause a problem because they'd be blocking the view of some of the audience. They wanted to figure out some way that all of the materials they were using didn't have to be in front of their puppet screen. Was there a way to arrange themselves, the puppets, and the light source so the audience did not see these? Ms. R helped them think about a way that they could accomplish their goal by extending some of their knowledge from prior learning experiences.

Over the course of the unit, the students and Ms. R had investigated several types of fabric. They had found that some types of cloth either let no light through (opaque), let all the light through (transparent), or let a little light through and caused it to disperse (translucent). She suggested they put the light source behind a light-colored, translucent, cloth shower curtain and see what it looked like from the audience side of the curtain. The students thought this might work. As they experimented with working from behind the translucent cloth, they recognized again that light traveled in a straight line. After investigating for a while, the students found that they could put their puppets in front of the light source, between the light and the backside of the curtain. They were delighted to find that from the audience side, their puppets looked like shadows on the curtain. They also found that the distance they created when they moved their puppets up and back in front of the light source made the puppets appear larger and smaller to the audience. This was a finding that some of the students had noted when investigating shadow play using the light boxes but was now rediscovered during the practice for the performance. To be sure *all* students had a chance to learn and perform, Ms. R put the children in groups of four. Each group created and performed a short skit with the puppets.

Ms. R recorded the program with a *video camera* so her students could later watch it, discuss the show, and identify how light worked in their show *(sparking a science conversation, applying new knowledge, making sense of their learning)*.

> Continuous assessment information can be shared by students critiquing themselves and each other: Planning and carrying out, and then debriefing, the puppet show was an authentic performance task that offered a host of additional opportunities for the collection of assessment data.

Ms. R's students were able to show the partnering class how the shadows were made and to discuss what they had learned about light in a double classroom forum after the show. An enthusiastic discussion ensued as the children in the other classroom made observations and asked questions of the students in Ms. R's class. The two teachers asked all students to report on "something that you have learned." Everyone wrote silently for five minutes and then read what they wrote by turning to a person sitting nearby but from the other room. A few students reported what they had learned from listening to these short readings. These responses were collected and the new learnings were added to their previous ideas. Here are examples of what Ms. R wrote based on the responses of the students:

Light passes through some materials.

Light can't be seen through some materials.

Light can be seen to an extent through some materials.

The shadows of objects become smaller when they're moved closer to a source of light.

Shadows of objects look bigger when they're moved farther away from the source of light.

> Continuous assessment data can be used to report student progress.

New ideas from the puppet show discussion were added to the previous concepts learned. The chart paper with each individual's ideas or learnings was kept. Ms. R had the students' journals with the students' ideas and diagrams over the life of the unit. She had her own notes, the photographs, the digital photos with students' ideas attached, as well as her notes from findings for each child from video clips and audiotapes.

All of these data allowed her to present information to parents and students at parent conferences (sometimes led by the student); it also provided a wealth of information for the school's standards-based report cards.

In this chapter we have shown you the importance of reflecting on and using the information you collect while your students are engaged in science in order to enhance student learning and to reflect on your own teaching practices. Once again, this practice is not limited to science, and, as you can see, would be beneficial to all disciplines.

The Journey 5

Challenges, Realities, and Advice

Implementing continuous assessment in the context of science inquiry reaps rewards for both you and your students. It also poses challenges, some of which are inherent in teaching, while others are more specific to this approach. Each section below describes a challenge teachers have experienced while working to implement science inquiry and continuous assessment, along with strategies they have devised for addressing the challenge. We encourage you to consider how these challenges resonate with you. Teachers: Which of these challenges are you experiencing? What have you tried? Might any of the strategies listed work in your setting? What challenges have you already overcome? How might you share your successful strategies with your colleagues? Professional developers: What challenges might your teachers be facing? How can you find out? How might you support your teachers to address the challenges?

CHALLENGE: HOW DO I MAKE TIME FOR SCIENCE INQUIRY AND CONTINUOUS ASSESSMENT?

> *"The roadblocks that I continue to meet are having time to plan and implement ideas and investigations."*
>
> —Elementary Teacher

> *"The biggest challenge I face is time. Inquiry takes a lot more classroom time than direct instruction."*
>
> —Elementary Teacher

As you implement inquiry and continuous assessment, you may feel that it takes more time than what you were doing before. This may be because you are trying something new. It also relates to the nature of science inquiry and continuous assessment. Engaging students in extended investigations does take more time than doing a demonstration of a phenomenon or having students read a chapter of a textbook. Videotaping students investigating and later viewing the video with students to help them reflect on their understanding does take more time than giving students a chapter test and grading it. The trade-off is in the learning. Research tells us that for students to experience change in conceptual understanding, they need time to test their ideas. They also need time to reflect with peers and the teacher on how their ideas change over time.

While it can feel overwhelming at first, teachers have found several ways to find time for science inquiry and continuous assessment. One strategy is to begin with small changes. Many teachers new to inquiry try just one or two extended investigations with their students in a year, usually focusing on topics they've taught many times and with which they are comfortable taking risks. As they become more familiar with the process, they try their new skills on other topics. In the same vein, teachers implementing continuous assessment suggest trying just one technique or tool at a time, one that you are comfortable with or excited about trying. Once you've tried it in a variety of ways, you will be ready to try a new one. It matters less which particular technique or tool you use, and more that you find one that is useful for your situation in terms of any equipment you might need, the time it takes to collect the data in the classroom, and time to reflect on the data afterward.

> *"I first started documenting by videotaping children in my classroom. I chose video cameras because I'm comfortable with them, so that would be a recommendation from me to anyone who's starting. To start with a tool that you like and you feel comfortable with and you want to know more about."*

> —Kindergarten Teacher

It also helps to remember that implementing continuous assessment can be as simple and efficient as sitting with a group of students, listening to their conversation, and reflecting on what you learn from it. Many teachers start this way, are amazed at what they learn about their students' understanding, and become motivated to find more time for continuous assessment as a result. The techniques of continuous assessment (sitting and listening closely, asking questions, etc.) are as important as the tools. Most teachers already employ many of these strategies, so their "start" with continuous assessment focuses on being more intentional about using the data they gather to inform their instruction, further student learning, and reflect on their teaching. It does take time to review continuous assessment data (e.g., to read student journals or review an audiotape), but the information you glean about students' understanding and your own teaching can save you time and enhance students' learning in the long run. Knowing mid-unit that students are not grasping a concept gives you time to adapt your teaching so that students can move forward the next day and get farther in their learning than they would have if you had waited to assess until the end of the unit.

Listed below are some more specific ways to make continuous assessment manageable time-wise (for more detail, see Chapter 3: "Techniques and Tools for Facilitating Inquiry and Collecting Student Data"):

- Involve parents, teaching assistants, and other volunteers in videotaping science time, taking notes as student groups investigate, or transcribing short audiotape excerpts.

- Not all audiotapes need to be transcribed. Listening to a tape while commuting or exercising is an efficient way to review the tape to gain information about where to go next with a group, or to help you isolate a short excerpt to play for the group or the class.

- While videotaping, make note of key moments as the action is occurring. When you review the tape, you can look for these moments (either for your own information or to share with students) instead of having to watch the entire tape.

- When taking notes, use a sticky note or computer label for each student. You can then transfer these notes to that student's page in a notebook or card file instead of rewriting them.

- When observing students, let go of the need to see every student every day. Collecting data about just a few students each day (while at the same time keeping track so that you know you've observed each student in the class over several days) makes it more manageable.

Other ways teachers have addressed the time issue include teaching fewer topics in a year and going into more depth with each, and working to integrate other subject areas with science. Many teachers integrate science with writing and social studies by tying the science to a real-world context or challenging students to take action based on what they've learned. For example, a fourth-grade class investigated the effects of road salt on plants, found that it had a negative effect, and wrote a letter to the town board suggesting that they stop using the salt. A member of the board visited the class and shared all the other issues involved in the decision to use salt (cost, availability, etc.), and the class had a lively debate and a meaningful introduction to economics and community decision making.

Another way to look at integration is to consider which skills from other subject areas students practice naturally as part of their science investigations. Many teachers report that their students are eager to write about their investigations, and that they write much more and, in some cases, with more facility in their science journals than at writing time. Most writing portfolio programs require that students write "procedural" pieces, and teachers find that students can use excerpts from their journals as the basis for these. Students also use numerous math skills as they investigate, including measuring of all kinds, collecting and organizing data in charts and graphs, interpreting those data, and drawing conclusions. One innovative new program is exploring integrating science into some of the published mathematics curricula (e.g., Investigations, Everyday Math, and Math Land). The program's developers and teachers have found some rich connections in such investigations as the geometry of structures, and patterns in the natural world. The way to save time with this type of integration is be intentional about the connections (and to resist duplicating your efforts in the other subject areas). Look at your writing portfolio requirements and consider how you might structure some science journal prompts to fulfill them. As you plan a science unit, think about your math curriculum requirements. Plan to teach some of the required math skills at a time when students will need to apply those same skills in their investigations. Teaching graphing using data students have collected in their science investigations not only saves you time (by teaching the math at the same time as the science), but gives students a more meaningful context within which to apply their skills.

CHALLENGE: HOW DO I INTEGRATE CONTINUOUS ASSESSMENT WITH TRADITIONAL TESTING?

"I have tried to model good inquiry practices but have a problem matching the inquiry process with demands of the sixth-grade science test."

—Sixth-Grade Teacher

"We need to work with parents to help them realize that there are other assessments besides paper tests."

—Fourth-Grade Teacher

Different assessments have different purposes, and result in different types of data (see Figure 1.1, "The Big Picture of Assessment," in Chapter 1). Standardized tests are meant to give a broad picture of learning and teaching across a district, state, or country. They are designed to be administered on a large scale in an efficient manner, and so can test only one type of knowledge, one quite removed from the type of learning involved in science inquiry:

> By their nature, it is difficult for large-scale, multiple choice tests to address important curriculum goals that require generative thinking, sustained effort over time, and effective collaboration. These important skills are better assessed by performance-based assessment methods, such as portfolios, computer simulations, oral presentations, and projects, which make greater demands on academic foundation, teamwork, and problem-solving skills than traditional paper-and-pencil assessments. (WestEd, 2000, pp. 2–3)

Standardized tests also test a student's knowledge at a certain point in time, the time at which the test is taken. Finally, the way the tests are administered (sitting for long periods of time, working alone, reading and answering questions) is often very far removed from the classroom context, especially classrooms where inquiry is the norm. Continuous assessment, in contrast, provides an ongoing picture of what is happening with individual students in the classroom. The tools and techniques capture evidence of student thinking and learning in a variety of ways throughout the phases of inquiry.

These two types of assessment have very different purposes and provide very different types of information. While standardized tests can raise a red flag if a student scores very poorly, for the most part they are meant to provide information about trends in student learning across a large population (e.g., district or state). Their primary purpose is to inform program decisions. Continuous assessment provides information about the individual and the class, and the data are used to inform instruction, enhance individual student learning, and inform the teacher's practice.

As you use continuous assessment strategies and techniques, you will gain confidence in your ability to describe your students' science development. As you administer required science tests, you will see firsthand what these tests are and are not able to measure. You will be able to compare what you know about your students (through continuous assessment) to what the test results tell you. As you become more clear about this distinction yourself, you can help parents and colleagues accurately interpret and learn from these two different sets of data.

You can also make an effort to help parents understand continuous assessment. Most parents grew up taking standardized tests, and trust the data they receive from them (however incomplete it may be for their individual child). By informing parents about what you value in science teaching and learning and by detailing your expectations and goals for students, you can help parents better understand continuous assessment. You can also share research that describes the benefits of continuous assessment. Black and Wiliam (1998), in their well-known review of research on formative assessment, state,

> Standards can be raised only by changes that are put into direct effect by teachers and pupils in classrooms. There is a firm body of evidence that formative assessment is an essential component of classroom work and that its development can raise standards of achievement. We know of no other way of raising standards for which such a strong prima facie case can be made. (p. 148)

CHALLENGE: HOW DO I
ACQUIRE MORE CONTENT KNOWLEDGE?

> *"I need more content training. I need to give myself the freedom to learn things that I have not had the opportunity to think of in the form of inquiry. Many science topics were not presented to me in a way that has helped me feel confident to teach them myself. With the inquiry model of teaching, new doors have opened to me. I want to revisit those parts of my own learning that feel 'above me' in some way.*
>
> *"I need training in more areas of science content and specific inquiry investigations that can accompany unit themes."*
>
> —Third-Grade Teacher

Once you begin to tease out and consider how to deepen students' thinking about concepts, you may feel the need to enrich your own conceptual understanding. Uncovering and understanding scientific concepts as an adult learner can build excitement, empathy, and a foundation for supporting students' emerging understanding. Remember, though, that developing solid understanding in the several science areas you may need to teach will take time.

Recent reform efforts and standards documents, including the National Science Education Standards, and Project 2061, recommend that districts and schools limit the numbers of topics teachers are responsible for at particular grade levels, and adopt comprehensive, research-based curricula (e.g., STC, Insights, FOSS, etc.). Both of these trends will help you address this content knowledge challenge. By teaching the same three or four topics year to year, and possibly having a standards-based curriculum supporting you, you will become more comfortable over time with the concepts inherent in the topics, and with how best to support students' investigation of the phenomena in ways that will increase their conceptual understanding. Also, when you know what you need to teach, you can choose professional development opportunities that allow you to become immersed as a learner in a specific content area for which you are responsible (e.g., the physics of motion or the geology of your region). Look for workshops and institutes that include practical experiences connected to a real-world context. Making the connection between the science you are learning and your everyday experiences will both deepen your understanding of the concepts and help you support your students to make such connections.

> *"I want more time to learn, enjoy, and make sense of content with the help of content specialists. Time to learn and question and explore before I am asked to apply my understanding to teaching. I also want time to explore my new learning of science concepts with students. I want them to see me as a learner and not as an encyclopedia. I'd like to develop an inquiry project that they see me explore and investigate: a learning lab for all of us."*
>
> —Fourth-Grade Teacher

CHALLENGE: HOW DO I MANAGE CONTINUOUS ASSESSMENT EFFECTIVELY?

On the surface, managing continuous assessment can seem challenging, especially in larger classes. As you try out the tools and techniques, you may feel frustrated trying to listen to or observe various groups, or trying to take notes or videotape while at the same time finding materials for students or ensuring that students are on task. There are probably days when even the most experienced teacher feels pulled in many directions like this—to some degree it is the nature of teaching. That said, teachers do have suggestions for making continuous assessment feel more manageable.

Turn Materials Management Over to Students

The more independent and effective students are in gathering and using materials, the more time you can spend observing and interacting with them about their learning. There are many things you can do to turn materials management over to your students. For example, organize and lay out materials in a particular place before an investigation session so that students know what is available to them, and know how and where to get what they need during the session. (Include materials students might need to extend an investigation, if you plan to give them that option.) Brainstorm guidelines with students as to appropriate use of the materials (and consequences for misuse) so they are clear about your expectations. This will help you do less "policing" during the investigation. If students have questions about materials or can't find something while they are investigating, encourage them to ask other students before they ask you. Often students can help each other solve these problems.

Trust That Students Can Be Productive On Their Own

Part of the struggle for many teachers implementing science inquiry and continuous assessment is in letting go of constantly directing students' learning. Yet when they allow investigation groups to function on their own, teachers report that they are amazed at how engaged and productive students can be. This does not happen instantly, however. You first need to build a classroom culture based on trust and respect for students' ideas—where there's an expectation that students will work independently, learn as a result, and share those learnings with peers and the teacher (see Chapter 2 for more detail). Once this expectation is established, you can feel more free to observe and assess just a few investigation groups per science class time, trusting that other groups are working productively without you. Each session you can keep track of which groups you visit, so that you can be sure to get to every group over time. You can also get a sense of where groups you didn't visit are in their investigations by having students write in their journals or share what they did that day in an end-of-the-session scientists' meeting or at the beginning of your next science session. Videotape and audiotape recordings are another way to monitor what went on in those groups. Of course there will be days when a group you weren't able to work with was less productive than it might have been had you been there. If expectations for the work to be accomplished that session were clear, you might ask that group to make up their missed work time at a break or after school. Or, you might simply meet with that group first thing the next science time to get them back on track.

Clarify Your Role

Be clear with students about your role as they are investigating. Let them know that you will be visiting some groups to learn about and document what they are doing, and to support them to move forward in their learning. Explain that this means that you want enough time to talk to each group, and that while you won't get to every group that session, you will get to all groups over time. Encourage students to interrupt you as infrequently as possible, and again, encourage them to ask classmates questions before asking you. One teacher uses the "three strikes rule"—students can't ask him a question unless they've first struck out with three classmates in trying to get the answer.

Over time students will learn to work more independently and you'll feel less of a time crunch around continuous assessment.

"One fall morning I invited my students to play with Oobleck (cornstarch and water mixture). I told them that I would be a silent reporter who listened and wrote down their ideas. Since it was the beginning of the year, I wanted them to get used to my not being the leader and question-answerer, but a quiet observer. My plan was to observe what students did and record exactly what they said. After a while, they ignored me and I could even catch their low-level mumblings, which were sometimes the most revealing. Students were fascinated by my stand-back position. They wanted to know what I was doing and what my notes would be used for. I told them I was documenting their learning for them, and planning our next steps."

—Third- and Fourth-Grade Teacher

CHALLENGE: HOW DO I HELP MY STUDENTS ENGAGE DEEPLY IN INQUIRY?

Encouraging students to extend their work time can be a problem. They say they are finished when they have actually only scratched the surface. They have been conditioned to treat science this way and need time to learn to be more rigorous.

There is no question that the approach to teaching, learning, and assessment proposed in this book is a change for many students (and teachers). If you and your students are new to inquiry and continuous assessment, give yourself at least a year to make the transition. Remember, and help students understand, that you are all learning to do things in a new way, and that change is a process, not an overnight occurrence. It takes a while to learn how to address the "I'm done, what shall I do now?" question. Thinking back to what was said in the section in Chapter 2 titled "The Foundation: Trust and Respect," you might think of your role when trying to address such a question. Try not to be caught up in being responsible for keeping your students *busy*. Rather this is an opportunity to have a conversation with genuine interest on your part about all the things they've tried and what they've found out to date. You'll be surprised what happens when you talk with and ask genuine questions about their work. New ideas come up and soon they'll be able to answer the question, "What would you like to do next to find out more about . . .?" Another strategy is to have them share their findings with another group or the whole group. In such discussions, their peers are bound to ask them questions that they can answer only by investigating further.

Try to routinely model science dispositions and clarify the expectations you have for your students. Engage students in developing learning goals and indicators of progress toward those goals. Provide multiple opportunities for them to practice and reflect on the skills and dispositions modeled and to express their understanding of the concepts in a nonthreatening, collegial atmosphere. Like you, your students need time and support to adjust to new ways of teaching and learning.

CHALLENGE: HOW DO I OBTAIN THE MATERIALS I NEED?

> *We discovered that teachers who are more reluctant to do science would stop because of lack of materials.*

> —Program Associate

You don't need expensive or obscure equipment to start science inquiry and continuous assessment. As you try out investigations with your students, you'll find that simple, familiar materials (e.g., eyedroppers, water, and wax paper; leaves and hand lenses) are often the best springboards. To assess, often all you need is a pen and paper. As you go deeper into investigations with your students, and/or become more interested in other continuous assessment tools, you will need a wider range of materials. If your school or district has purchased kit-based curricula, you may find all the science materials you need in the kits. However, many schools find it challenging to continually replenish the consumable materials in the kits, and/or to keep the kits complete. You may also find that you want additional materials so that you and your students can extend investigations beyond the materials provided in the kit. Teachers have found many ways to secure the science inquiry and continuous assessment materials they need.

Many teachers find that planning is key to obtaining materials. They look at their budgets, and consider what they need for the upcoming year and what they might put off for a year. They also connect with other teachers and administrators to discuss what supplies might be bought (through existing budgets or through grant funds) for the school to share (e.g., hand lenses, Polaroid film, a digital camera).

Teachers have also had success scrounging for materials. While this may sound time-consuming, it doesn't have to be. For example, at the beginning of the year or a few weeks before starting a unit, make a list of materials you need (e.g., plastic containers, foil, film, blank audio or video cassettes) and send a request home to parents (older students could write such a note themselves). Alternatively, ask a parent or volunteer to coordinate a schoolwide materials drive or to solicit materials from local organizations and businesses (e.g., hospitals, office supply stores, hardware stores). Having a good set of materials before you start a unit can save you time and frustration as students start investigating. If, once the unit is under way, students develop their own investigations that require materials other than what you have, hand the responsibility for finding the materials over to them. This challenges students to consider whether or not their investigation design is reasonable and can be accomplished with readily available materials—an important consideration for any scientist.

CHALLENGE: HOW DO I GAIN
PARENT INVOLVEMENT AND SUPPORT?

"Many adults have never inquired into science materials and so they don't have a sense of materials themselves and haven't made their own meaning from those materials. So they don't have a clue sometimes what students are talking about. That is unnerving and sometimes parents want to regain control by having students learn the way they did because that's what they understand. So I think that it's good to think about moving from formative assessment in the classroom to how to report that out to families in a way that makes sense. What we have done is have students be a part of parent conferences so that parents can really hear their children articulate what they have learned, and the result is that parents feel more comfortable with less formal assessments."

—Elementary Principal

Many parents, like teachers, did not have opportunities to engage in inquiry investigations while they were in school. Nor was it likely that they were assessed through continuous assessment. As a result, they may perceive your program to lack structure and/or content. There are many ways to help parents to first understand, and then support your program. A good place to start is to explain what your goals are for your students in terms of science concepts, processes, and dispositions, and to share documents that detail and support these, such as Figure 2.2 in Chapter 2 or excerpts from local or national standards documents. Explain how you keep track of student progress in these areas through the tools and techniques of continuous assessment. Share samples of continuous assessment data, and explain what you understand from them about their child's progress.

It is also very helpful to get parents involved in science inquiry and continuous assessment firsthand, to show them "what it looks like" through video, and/or to give students concrete ways to share their learning with parents. Consider the following suggestions:

• Set up an "inquiry investigation station" in your room during the traditional open house or other events when parents come to the school, and invite parents to explore the materials.

- Host a special event (e.g., a "Family Science Night") during which students and parents engage in investigations together.

- Ask parents to help you collect continuous assessment data in the classroom. Be clear about what you want them to capture (e.g., students' use of measuring tools or ability to work collaboratively), and how you want them to use a particular tool (e.g., taking Polaroid photographs and having students annotate them, or interviewing students on tape). Find a few minutes after the session to talk with parents about what they learned from their experience, and/or to answer any questions.

> *"Time for me to record children's thinking is limited, so I decided to involve a parent volunteer to help me collect and record information about each child's present knowledge and what they wanted to learn about light. We then asked them at the end of the unit to tell what they knew about light and to explain one of their investigations. We typed their ideas on the computer and they later added an illustration to further clarify their statements. This before-and-after data gathering gave me new insights about my students' thinking, and helped the parent better understand what her child was doing in science."*
>
> —First- and Second-Grade Teacher

- At conference time, set up a VCR and show footage of students investigating for parents to watch while they wait for their appointment with you.

- Include students in parent conferences and have them explain (using actual materials, journal writings, annotated photographs, etc.) how their understanding of a concept changed from the beginning to the end of an investigation.

- Send videos home with students so they can watch them with their parents and talk about what was happening in their investigation during the clip.

- Send short notes home (students can write these as well as teachers) noting a student's progress in science concepts, processes, and dispositions with specific examples that refer to ongoing investigations.

- Assign projects (that can be completed with everyday materials) for students to do with parents or caregivers. (If you know students do not have the materials at home, set up a table or box of materials from which all students can choose what they need.)

"An important part of our science investigations is the home/school connection. I have seen excellent results come from assigning a home project for children to do with their parents, then bringing the finished project into school to share with the class. For instance, during a unit on sound, the home project was to make an "instrument" that produced sound. These family projects allow children to discuss what is happening at school with their families, learning new skills and gathering more information from family members."

—Second-Grade Teacher

By trying out some of these ideas, you may not only gain parents' support, but their involvement in your classroom as well, which can only strengthen your program and benefit your students.

Every day, you face challenges in teaching and assessment. The challenges we discuss in this chapter, as you know, aren't all unique to the discipline of science. Much of the advice here is applicable to all disciplines. Our suggestion always in incorporating inquiry and continuous assessment is to go slowly and to start with what is comfortable for you. Over time you may find that trying this approach isn't really something new, but just a matter of tweaking what you already do well.

For support from the National Science Education Standards in addressing these challenges see Resource B, Table B.4, "NSES: Changing Emphases for Programs" and Table B.5, "NSES: Changing Emphases for Systems."

Continuous Assessment and Professional Growth   6

"My standards for professional development have changed. If I am truly going to implement new strategies in my classroom, then I need the time and commitment to discuss my progress with other professionals, receive feedback on my attempts thus far, and plan my next steps. My learning takes place over time and requires reflection and support. My classroom experiences in science and assessment support my professional development."

—Elementary Teacher

"The type of professional development that happens with this type of assessment is an inquiry into itself. You are asking questions of the practice, you are getting data, you are then saying hopefully to some colleagues, 'are you noticing this too,' and I just think that changes the whole arena of professional development."

—Senior Consultant

Thus far you've been reading about various aspects of continuous assessment—the context in which it takes place, what it might look like, tools and techniques, how to analyze the data, and so on. In this chapter we describe continuous assessment from the point of view of professional development. We focus on the type of professional development you gain by reflecting on your practice on your own and/or with a group of peers, and what you might look for in a more formal setting such as a course or an institute. These topics, along with a professional development vignette from our own work, help bring this important issue alive.

Educators at all levels are redefining the character and role of professional development in schools. Research supports the vision of the professional development context as one in which teachers work with one another and with their own students in learning communities. As you read this chapter and plan ways to incorporate continuous assessment into your practice, you may want to consider the professional development that will best support your own and your students' growth.

CONTINUOUS ASSESSMENT AS PROFESSIONAL DEVELOPMENT

Just as you use students' everyday experiences as the basis for improving and tracking their development, your everyday classroom experiences can become an important vehicle for your own professional growth. As you strive to better understand and guide students' learning, you will find yourself reflecting on your teaching strategies and how they impact that learning. You might ask yourself, *"What can I do to encourage students to plan their investigations more carefully?"* or *"What experiences can I provide for students to challenge their misconceptions?"*

As explained in Chapter 4, you can analyze the assessment data you gather (about students) through this lens of personal, professional growth. Here are some suggestions:

• Watch video clips or listen to audiotapes with particular questions about your teaching in mind (e.g., lines of questioning, interactions with different students, your role in discussions, how the lesson models inquiry).

> *"I feel that there is so much I need to learn more about inquiry science but I'm willing to just take the chances and learn as I go and let it become a growth process for me."*

> —Fifth-Grade Teacher

• Review a videotape or audiotape (or read a transcription) of a class discussion to analyze your facilitation skills. Did your interventions help to open or unintentionally close discussion? Did you feed students information and directions, or did you ask productive questions to spark their thinking? Were there times you didn't intervene when you should have (e.g., when the discussion moved to unrelated topics)? How might you improve your facilitation skills?

• Ask a colleague to visit your classroom, watch a video, listen to an audiotape with you, or just listen to you as you relate the day's activities, and share his or her impressions or comment on particular issues about your teaching you want to address. What ideas does he or she have for refining your practice?

"My team teacher, Susan, comes in and videotapes three times a year. Then we sit down and look at the videotape together, and talk about what's happening. I have certain ideas that might need somebody else to kind of juggle around and say, 'Well, did you think of looking at it this way?' Susan has really helped me to do that."

—Kindergarten Teacher

• Review your observation notes from several class sessions and determine how useful they are to you. Are you recording enough detail? Too much? Do your notes reflect pure observations or interpretations? Do notes from several days ago still make sense? Are you learning what you had hoped from your notes about students' progress toward learning goals? Would a different documentation tool give you more accurate or complete information? Perhaps a digital photograph might help in capturing a certain classroom moment and the actions of a student or group of students.

• Watch a video clip to become more aware of your actions and movement around the room. For instance, do you sit with or stand over students? How much time do you spend interacting with students about their learning compared with time spent gathering materials and keeping students on task?

• Review student journal entries. Is there variety in your journal assignments (e.g., asking students to respond to a question, draw a diagram, write a letter to a younger child explaining a concept)? Are you learning what you had expected from students' entries? Do you write back to your students? Do different assignments provide you with different information? Do different students respond better to different assignments?

"My experiences with continuous assessment—with the encouragement to practice classroom research, peer sharing sessions and inquiry—has been my most significant professional development experience in twenty-plus years of teaching. It is so rewarding to work with other professionals who are asking questions about the practices of teaching and assessment; and, more so, who seek solutions. By actually keying in on what was happening in the classroom, I became more motivated to be a better teacher. The process became more than just teaching. My experiences have instilled the drive to discover the best teaching and to implement it."

—Elementary Teacher

Reflecting, Analyzing, and Learning With Colleagues

"What I'm hungry for are more sessions where a group of teachers is experimenting, reporting out to each other, and relating stories and questions from our own up-to-the-minute, red-hot science time with kids."

—Elementary Teacher

While it is helpful to analyze your teaching and your students' development on your own, another very effective forum for reflection is with other teachers who are also implementing inquiry and using formative assessment practices. The support and feedback that you'll give to each other is invaluable and key to the personalized growth that comes from this type of professional development. Consider how you might create some of these opportunities for reflecting with colleagues in your unique context:

• If there are other teachers in your school interested in science inquiry and/or continuous assessment, consider setting up or joining a study group around a specific topic. The group might share classroom experiences, analyze student work, discuss readings, and so on. In her outstanding book, *Using Data/Getting Results: A Practical Guide for School Improvement in Mathematics and Science,* Nancy Love includes two "Data Tools" that your group might use as a first step in establishing guidelines by which you can examine and reflect on student work (Love, 2002, pp. 376-377). These guidelines are known as "protocols" and may help to give your support group a helpful structure with which you can best reflect on students and their work as well as on teaching practices.

• If you team teach, consider setting aside time to plan, review student work, and reflect on science experiences with your team members.

"You've heard of the old adage that two heads are better than one? This was especially true as my team teacher and I supported each other in our attempts to sort out and collect different types of evidence that yes, indeed, showed we had good science learning going on in our classrooms. In some ways it's great to have somebody who doesn't know your kids, because her ideas are very different. She'll say, 'Oh, but you know what though? They got to it here!' And I would have missed that if I had been the only person listening."

—Second-Grade Teacher

• Consider using release time to co-teach or observe in another classroom. Ask a colleague to provide some coaching around a particular problem or teaching practice. For instance, he or she might observe you facilitating a science session, then share observations on your questioning strategies and their impact on students.

- If you are working with a professional development provider, ask for direct classroom support. This might mean mentoring or coaching, co-teaching a session, co-planning a unit, or finding appropriate materials.

"The opportunity to share experiences with my peers as well as to assist them in their own inquiries has given validity to what we all are doing."

—Elementary Teacher

Support From Professional Development Standards

As you look both within and beyond the classroom for ways to grow in your understanding of and facility with continuous assessment, you might want to review the findings about effective professional growth published by national education organizations. Gaining this knowledge can inspire you to learn about inquiry and assessment, be it for science or any other discipline. You will find this knowledge helpful when seeking support from administrators, parents, and colleagues. You will seek (and demand!) professional development opportunities that include elements of these standards. Take a minute to review the *National Science Education Standards (NSES)* followed by a description of a model of our own professional development experience. In these examples, you will find that the kind of ongoing professional development that occurs when you use continuous assessment is consistent with what is advocated by experts in the field (Figure 6.1).

National Science Education Standards

In 1996, the National Academy of Sciences, working with leading national science education organizations, published the *National Science Education Standards.* This publication features a chapter titled, "Standards for Professional Development for Teachers of Science." Although these standards are primarily intended to inform anyone who provides professional development, teachers are urged to use the standards as criteria for selecting and designing activities for their own professional growth. In Figure 6.1, the professional development standards are expressed on a "less emphasis, more emphasis" continuum. We have added a third column with short descriptors of practices that are consistent with continuous assessment *and* supportive of the professional development standards for science teachers (see Resource B, Table B.6, "NSES: Changing Emphases for Professional Development").

Figure 6.1

National Science Education Standards for Professional Development &		
Descriptors of Professional Growth Opportunities when used with Continuous Assessment		
Less Emphasis On . . .	**More Emphasis On . . .**	**Professional Growth with CA**
Transmission of teaching knowledge and skills by lectures	Inquiry into teaching and learning	*The classroom as the site for collecting data used to drive your professional growth*
Learning science by lecture and reading	Learning science through investigation and inquiry	*Learning science through investigation and reflection on continuous assessment data*
Separation of science and teaching knowledge	Integration of science and teaching knowledge	*Integration of science, inquiry, and teaching knowledge and practices via continuous assessment*
Separation of theory and practice	Integration of theory and practice in school settings	*Integration of theory and practice informed by continuous assessment data*
Individual learning	Collegial and collaborative learning	*Collegial and collaborative learning among teachers and students through review of continuous assessment data*
Fragmented, one-shot sessions	Long-term coherent plans	*Long-term planning for practicing and learning from inquiry and assessment*
Courses and workshops	A variety of professional development activities	*Using classroom practice and continuous assessment to guide choices for individual professional development in science*
Reliance on external expertise	Mix of internal and external expertise	*Mix, with emphasis on internal expertise developed through reflection on continuous assessment data individually and with colleagues*
Staff developers as educators	Staff developers as facilitators, consultants, and planners	*Staff developers as co-inquirers, facilitators, consultants*
Teacher as technician	Teacher as intellectual, reflective practitioner	*Teacher as reflective practitioner who uses classroom data to improve practice and student learning*
Teacher as consumer of knowledge about teaching	Teacher as producer of knowledge about teaching	*Teacher as producer and sharer of practice-based knowledge about teaching emerging from continuous assessment*
Teacher as follower	Teacher as leader	*Teacher as professional developer for self and others*
Teacher as individual based in a classroom	Teacher as a member of a collegial professional community	*Teacher as member of local collegial group focused on learning through continuous assessment*

Source: Reprinted with permission from the *National Science Education Standards*, copyright 1996 by the National Academy of Sciences. Courtesy of the National Academies Press, Washington, D.C.

AN EXAMPLE OF EFFECTIVE PROFESSIONAL DEVELOPMENT

An elementary school (K-8 of approximately 600 students) decided to engage its faculty in an effort to improve science teaching and learning. In April, our team met with the science task force, including the assistant principal and twelve classroom teachers. A lively discussion took place about the kind of professional development that would be appropriate for the school. *"This first meeting is what we call the pre-institute mode, in which teachers and administrators become active participants in the planning. When we work* with *them instead of coming in and doing a program* for *them, we create a more positive and collaborative learning environment. The teachers have a real investment,"* says Project Director Maura Carlson.

The model we agreed on included a four-day institute at the beginning of summer and two follow-up days at the end of August just before school started up again. The program would continue throughout the school year with three scheduled after-school inservice programs and 10 days set aside for visits to the teachers in their classrooms or during a planning period.

Sixteen teachers as well as the principal and assistant principal were involved in the project. "Over the years, we have found that having the principal, and in this case the assistant principal as well, involved makes an important statement about the importance of science in the school," Maura says. "The teachers see their administrators working with us, and feel supported as the science initiative unfolds. The result is greater success all around, as things take hold in the schools."

The Institute

This initiative was guided by our beliefs that for teachers to feel comfortable teaching inquiry-based science and conducting continuous assessment, they first need to experience inquiry for themselves as adult learners, understand the concepts of the science they are teaching, see continuous assessment modeled, and have the opportunity to practice and to reflect on their integration of inquiry and assessment in their classrooms with support from mentors and peers.

These goals become the basis for the "strands" of the institute. The "Inquiry Strand" takes teachers at their current level of experience and introduces learning science through an inquiry-based approach. Teachers raise questions within the context of a concept area (in this case the science of "fluids: water and air"), and plan and carry out an investigation to help answer their questions. The findings resulting from their investigations are shared. With input from their peers and the support of the facilitators, these teachers are able to make sense of the concept.

Running concurrently with the "Inquiry Strand" is the "Continuous Assessment Strand." In the continuous assessment strand, facilitators model the use of formative assessment strategies and tools to observe and gather data regarding each teacher's progress in his or her inquiries. The facilitators then use those data to offer immediate feedback, to plan for the next lesson, or to make adjustments in their own teaching practices. In other words, they model what they hope teachers will do when they are teaching their students. They also make transparent and explicit exactly what they are modeling. Participants are given time to ask questions about both the science concepts and practices they are learning as well as the methods that the professional developers are using as they teach.

The science topic under investigation by the teachers is the heart of the third strand, the "Content Strand." In this strand, teachers use their investigation findings, along with the information provided by the facilitators and the assisting scientist, to further understand the concepts of the current topic.

The "Sustained Support Strand" continues throughout the school year. As the school year approaches, we challenge participants to consider how they might apply these new strategies of science education in their classrooms. We are also a continuous resource for the participants, offering follow-up meetings and on-site support throughout the school year. We gladly co-teach in their classrooms if asked. We even provide a professional development newsletter to broadcast "how it's going" to participants and to the rest of the school staff and parents.

Our Approach

The approach for each institute is based on trust and respect for teachers' ideas and input. By starting off this way, our center team models our own beliefs and principles about teaching, learning, and assessment as we invite the teachers to become involved in their own inquiry as adult learners. We listen to teachers' ideas, just as a teacher would listen to students' ideas, and we model assessment strategies and tools just as they will use these strategies and tools with their own students. *"Many teachers at the elementary level have a degree of fear associated with learning and teaching science,"* says Maura. *"Yet, they are already experienced teachers. They know how to look around a classroom and recognize good reading or math skills, but with science it can be more challenging, because many often don't know what to look for as indicators of quality science. Our job is to help them experience being a scientist, to develop with them indicators of what they would see and expect their students to be learning and doing, and to provide tools and strategies for documenting and using assessment data."*

As teachers experience inquiry for themselves as learners, see continuous assessment modeled, and deepen their own content knowledge, they begin to consider what they'd like to bring back to their own classrooms. They have more confidence in what science learning and teaching can be and what to look for as they assess student progress. *"This confidence puts our teachers at ease, and the students can sense that,"* says Maura.

Planning and Reflecting at the August Follow-Up

The next important step in the process is planning and reflecting. Here the teachers change hats from student to teacher, and spend time integrating inquiry and continuous assessment into their curriculum for the next year. *"We try to make a distinction between when we are talking with the teachers as learners, and when we are talking with them as teachers for their students,"* says Maura. *"So throughout the institute we were making a point of them learning for themselves. Now that we've completed the initial work, we tell them it's now time to think about their students' learning."* Some of the questions we started with included things like: What science do you want to start with this year? What aspect of inquiry and formative assessment intrigues you enough to try it out this fall? What kind of support can we give you?

We encourage the teachers to focus on the first unit they are going to teach, and what assessment tool they would use to gather information. Some of the participants want assistance in gathering materials and background information. Other teachers are preparing units on topics like "light" or "the desert" and want ideas about how to integrate inquiry and assessment with these topics. For example, a teacher who was developing a unit on the desert worked with Maura to come up with investigations on heating and measuring the temperature of sand as compared to something more stable, like water. *"I often tell the teachers that you can take a recipe activity like making a heat detector, and add a little twist to make it more inquiry-oriented."*

Our Continuing Relationship With the School

In a way, this institute was just the beginning of a longer-term relationship between our Center for Science Education and Professional Development and the elementary school. Over the following year, we visited the school regularly, and worked with the teachers both individually and in groups as they slowly integrated continuous assessment into their teaching. We also had three large-group follow-up sessions of three hours each. *"This isn't something that you just learn and that's the end of it,"* says Maura. *"What happens is that teachers start with one inquiry or continuous assessment tool and try that out. Once they're comfortable with that, they add another. So the key thing is that we continue to support them over time so that when their challenges come up, we are there to help."*

PROFESSIONAL DEVELOPMENT RECOMMENDATIONS

Students cannot achieve high levels of learning and performance unless teachers, principals, and other school employees are continuously learning. Staff development not only includes high-quality, ongoing training with intensive follow-up and support, but also other growth-promoting processes such as study groups, action research, and peer coaching, to name a few. (National Staff Development Council, n.d.)

The following recommendations summarize what effective professional development in science inquiry and continuous assessment can look like. Some of the ideas apply to your classroom learning and others to off-site professional development experiences. Refer to these reminders as you reflect on and advocate for your own professional growth, and as you consider new professional experiences. If you are a professional development provider, you might want to read through these suggestions and compare them to your practices and your beliefs about teaching and supporting teachers.

- Use your daily classroom experiences to learn about your students' thinking and abilities and the impact of your teaching strategies. Use the formative assessment data you gather to help you advance student learning and improve your own teaching practices.
- Seek opportunities to engage in content-rich inquiry as an adult learner and to see continuous assessment modeled.
- Reflect on what you most value in teaching and learning. Explore how these core beliefs align with national and local teaching and learning standards, and how they clarify a vision to drive your instruction.
- Seek professional development opportunities that provide long-term support. Look for experiences that allow you to pursue in-depth, compelling questions about science teaching, learning, and assessment with sustained support over time.
- Seek opportunities to collaborate, explore new ideas, and share experiences and dilemmas with colleagues. These collaborations can inspire and support your professional growth.
- Build administrative support by sharing your experience of the benefits of classroom-based professional development.

CONTEXT FOR PROFESSIONAL DEVELOPMENT

Professional development can take many forms, depending on the needs of the educator. To support lasting changes in teacher practice, we advocate sustained professional development in a variety of contexts. The contexts range from your own classroom as a site for professional development, to teacher peer groups and workshop experiences with providers who model the national standards for teaching and professional development. Here are some other examples of such contexts:

- An early awareness meeting with teachers, science committees, and administrators to help identify issues that need to be addressed to support a comprehensive and successful implementation of a K-12 science program.

• A one- or two-day session in which participants engage in the initial stages of a cycle of inquiry, see formative assessment modeled, and consider the types of support they might need to go further.

• A multiday local institute for teachers, during which participants experience a full cycle of inquiry as adult learners, see continuous assessment modeled, and increase their knowledge of a particular content/concept area such as motion, light, fluids.

• Support sessions over time for institute participants with meetings, classroom visits, and phone, e-mail and Web site conversations. Participants share successes and challenges in implementing inquiry and assessment in their work and receive feedback, support, ideas, and resources from peers and professional development providers.

> *"Practicing continuous assessment as my own professional development addresses both student learning and my adult learning and thinking. Through reflecting on how I approach my own learning, discussing connections to pedagogy with other peers, and continuing to value and learn science content, I get a much fuller and more useful experience than with most other so-called 'inservice' models."*
>
> —Elementary Teacher

> *". . . it's formative assessment, but it's formative assessment of the teacher enabling the students to change their practice. But it's also the teacher being able to reflect on what pedagogical changes she's had to make in order to change the practice of the student, so they are doing this dance together back and forth over time."*
>
> —Doris Ash, Staff Member,
> Institute for Inquiry, the Exploratorium

Resource A

Techniques, Tools, and Uses of Continuous Assessment

Table A.1   Techniques of Continuous Assessment

Techniques	*What You Will See*
Sitting and listening closely	Teachers watch the behavior of the students at work and listen to their conversations.
Close-in, participant observation	Teachers listen closely and may ask questions during conversations to clarify details about what students are doing and what they are finding out but otherwise do not interfere.
Purposeful questioning	Teachers ask open-ended questions that enable students to reflect, clarify, and explain their thinking and actions and give their point of view during investigations.
Sharing new material/information	Teachers give students new materials or information to help them move deeper in their inquiry.
Sparking science conversations	Teachers structure opportunities for whole-class and individual conversations to explore the learning occurring through the inquiry.
Student self-assessment	Students conduct routine reflection.

Table A.2   Tools of Continuous Assessment

Tools	What You Will See
Note taking and observation checklists	Teachers use pen and paper to record their observations of student actions and words.
Videotaping	Teachers use video cameras to record brief but meaningful phases of student investigations. Students and teachers review the tapes to spark discussion, deepen the inquiry, and better understand the learning.
Audiotaping	Teachers set up tape recorders near students and record their conversations as small group inquiry occurs. Transcriptions can then be used with students to reflect on student thinking and determine new directions.
Photography—digital, 35 mm, or Polaroid	Teachers take photographs of students at work during defining moments. Students and teachers discuss and write about the science occurring behind the captured images to deepen the inquiry.
Student journals	Students record observations, thoughts, and data during inquiry. Teachers may offer purposeful questions as prompts.

Table A.3   The Purposes and Uses of Continuous Assessment

. . . serves instruction while monitoring growth	• Provides an accurate picture of student capabilities observed and recorded over time • Helps teacher determine next steps to support student growth immediately and over the long term • Captures what students are doing and thinking, with and without adult intervention
. . . enhances student learning	• Catalyzes "deeper" thinking and understanding as students reflect on their investigative processes and experiences • Provides timely feedback throughout investigations; encourages students to expand their thinking, modify investigations, and revise ideas • Helps students recognize what is valued so they can identify their own and peers' growth and can work toward concrete learning goals
. . . enables teachers' professional growth	• By striving to better understand and guide students' thinking and learning, teachers become more reflective about their practices and hone their teaching strategies • As a result of looking closely and of sharing experiences with colleagues, teachers develop new perspectives on how teaching and learning interact
. . . provides information to report students' progress	• Provides an accurate picture of students' growth in science and how their understanding, abilities, and dispositions change over time • Conveys expectations to students, parents, other teachers, administrators, and the community • Enables teachers/students to communicate evidence of learning to themselves, one another, parents, other teachers, administrators, and others

Resource B

National Science Education Standards Changing Emphases Summaries

Table B.1   NSES: Changing Emphases for Assessment

Less emphasis on . . .	*More emphasis on . . .*
Assessing what is easily measured	Assessing what is most highly valued
Assessing discrete knowledge	Assessing rich, well-structured knowledge
Assessing scientific knowledge	Assessing scientific understanding and reasoning
Assessing to learn what students do not know	Assessing to learn what students do understand
Assessing only achievement	Assessing achievement and opportunity to learn
End-of-term assessment by teachers	Students engaged in ongoing assessment of their work and that of others
Development of external assessments by measurement experts alone	Teachers involved in the development of external assessments

Reprinted with permission from the *National Science Education Standards.* Copyright 1996 by the National Academy of Sciences. Courtesy of the National Academies Press, Washington, D.C.

Table B.2   NSES: Changing Emphases for Contents

Less emphasis on . . .	*More emphasis on . . .*
Knowing scientific facts and information	Understanding scientific concepts and developing abilities of inquiry
Studying subject matter disciplines for their own sake	Learning subject matter disciplines in the context of inquiry, technology, science in personal and social perspectives, and history and nature of science
Separating science knowledge and science process	Integrating all aspects of science content
Covering many science topics	Studying a few fundamental science concepts
Implementing inquiry as a set of processes	Implementing inquiry as instructional strategies, abilities, and ideas to be learned
Activities that demonstrate and verify science content	Activities that investigate and analyze science questions
Investigations confined to one class period	Investigations over extended periods of time
Process skills out of context	Process skills in context
Emphasis on individual process skills such as observation or inference	Using multiple process skills— Manipulation, cognitive, procedural
Getting an answer	Using evidence and strategies for developing or revising an explanation
Science as exploration and experiment	Science as argument and explanation
Providing answers to questions about science content	Communicating science explanations
Individuals and groups of students analyzing and synthesizing data without defending a conclusion	Groups of students often analyzing and synthesizing data after defending conclusions
Doing a few investigations in order to leave time to cover large amounts of content	Doing more investigations in order to develop understanding, ability, values of inquiry, and knowledge of science content
Concluding inquiries with the result of the experiment	Applying the results of experiments to scientific arguments and explanations
Management of materials and equipment	Management of ideas and information
Private communication of student ideas and conclusions to teacher	Public communication of student ideas and work to classmates

Table B.3   NSES: Changing Emphases for Teaching

Less emphasis on . . .	*More emphasis on . . .*
Treating all students alike and responding to the group as a whole	Understanding and responding to individual student's interests, strengths, experiences, and needs
Rigidly following curriculum	Selecting and adapting curriculum
Focusing on student acquisition of information	Focusing on student understanding and use of scientific knowledge, ideas, and inquiry processes
Presenting scientific knowledge through lecture, text, and demonstration	Guiding students in active and extended scientific inquiry
Asking for recitation of acquired knowledge	Providing opportunities for scientific discussion and debate among students
Testing students for factual information at the end of the unit or chapter	Continuously assessing student understanding
Maintaining responsibility and authority	Sharing responsibility for learning with students
Supporting competition	Supporting a classroom community with cooperation, shared responsibility, and respect
Working alone	Working with other teachers to enhance the science program

Reprinted with permission from the *National Science Education Standards*. Copyright 1996 by the National Academy of Sciences. Courtesy of the National Academies Press, Washington, D.C.

Table B.4   NSES: Changing Emphases for Programs

Less emphasis on . . .	*More emphasis on . . .*
Developing science programs at different grade levels independently of one another	Coordinating the development of the K-12 science program across grade levels
Using assessments unrelated to curriculum and teaching	Aligning curriculum, teaching, and assessment
Maintaining current resource allocations for books	Allocating resources necessary for hands-on inquiry teaching aligned with the *Standards*
Textbook- and lecture-driven curriculum	Curriculum that supports the *Standards* and includes a variety of components, such as laboratories emphasizing inquiry and field trips
Broad coverage of unconnected factual information	Curriculum that includes natural phenomena and science-related social issues that students encounter in everyday life
Treating science as a subject isolated from other school subjects	Connecting science to other school subjects, such as mathematics and social studies
Science learning opportunities that favor one group of students	Providing challenging opportunities for all students to learn science
Limiting hiring decisions to the administration	Involving successful teachers of science in the hiring process
Maintaining the isolation of teachers	Treating teachers as professionals whose work requires opportunities for continual learning and networking
Supporting competition	Promoting collegiality among teachers as a team to improve the school

Table B.5   Changing Emphases for Systems

Less emphasis on . . .	*More emphasis on . . .*
Technical, short-term, inservice workshops	Ongoing professional development to support teachers
Policies unrelated to *Standards*-based reform	Policies designed to support changes called for in the *Standards*
Purchase of textbooks based on traditional topics	Purchase or adoption of curriculum aligned with the *Standards* and on a conceptual approach to science teaching, including support for hands-on science materials
Standardized tests and assessments unrelated to *Standards*-based programs and practices	Assessments aligned with the *Standards*
Administration determining what will be involved in improving science education	Teacher leadership in improvement of science education
Authority at upper levels of educational system	Authority for decisions at level of implementation
School board ignorance of science education program	School board support of improvements aligned with the *Standards*
Local union contracts that ignore changes in curriculum, instruction, and assessment	Local union contracts that support improvements indicated by the *Standards*

Table B.6   NSES: Changing Emphases for Professional Development

Less emphasis on . . .	More emphasis on . . .
Transmission of teaching knowledge and skills by lecture	Inquiry into teaching and learning
Learning science by lecture and reading	Learning science through investigation and inquiry
Separation of science and teaching knowledge	Integration of science and teaching knowledge
Separation of theory and practice	Integration of theory and practice in school settings
Individual learning	Collegial and collaborative learning
Fragmented, one-shot sessions	Long-term, coherent plans
Courses and workshops	A variety of professional development activities
Reliance on external expertise	Mix of internal and external expertise
Staff developers as educators	Staff developers as facilitators, consultants, and planners
Teacher as technician	Teacher as intellectual, reflective practitioner
Teacher as consumer of knowledge about teaching	Teacher as producer of knowledge about teaching
Teacher as follower	Teacher as leader
Teacher as individual based in a classroom	Teacher as a member of a collegial professional community
Teacher as target of change	Teacher as source and facilitator of change

Reprinted with permission from the *National Science Education Standards*. Copyright 1996 by the National Academy of Sciences. Courtesy of the National Academies Press, Washington, D.C.

References

American Association for the Advancement of Science (AAAS). (1993). *Benchmarks for science literacy.* New York: Oxford University Press.

Black, P., & Wiliam, D. (1998, October). Inside the black box: Raising standards through classroom assessment. *Phi Delta Kappan, 80*(2).

Bybee, R., Buchwald, C. E., Crissman, S., Heil, D. R., Kuerbis, P. J., Matsumoto, C., & McInerney, J. D. (1989). *Science and technology education for the elementary years: Frameworks for curriculum and instruction.* Andover, MA: The National Center for Improving Science Education, The NETWORK Inc.

The Center for Science Education and Professional Development for Learning Innovations (Producer). (2001). *The essence of continuous assessment* [Videotape]. Williston, VT: WestEd. (Available from WestEd, Williston, VT 05495)

Clarke, G. (1998). *Riding the wave of students' conceptual understanding: using continuous assessments in an inquiry science classroom.* Unpublished manuscript, Saint Michael's College, Colchester, VT.

Foundations: Inquiry thoughts, views and strategies for the K-5 classroom: A monograph for professionals in science, mathematics, and technology education (NSF Publication 99-148). Available on the World Wide Web at http://www.her.nsf.gov/esie/publications

Harlen, W. (1983). *Science: Guides to assessment in education.* London: Macmillan Education.

Harlen, W. (1985). *Primary science . . . taking the plunge: How to teach science more effectively for ages 5 to 12* (2nd ed.). Portsmouth, NH: Heinemann.

Loucks-Horsley, S., Hewson, P. W., Love, N., & Stiles, K. E. (1998). *Designing professional development for teachers of science and mathematics.* Thousand Oaks, CA: Corwin Press.

National Research Council. (1996). *National science education standards.* Washington, D.C.: National Academy Press.

National Research Council. (2001). *Classroom assessment and the national science education standards* (edited by J. M. Atkin, P. Black, & J. Coffey). Washington, D.C.: National Academy Press. Available on the World Wide Web at http://www.nap.edu/catalog/9847.html

ADDITIONAL READING

Doris, E. (1991). *Doing what scientists do: Children learn to investigate their world.* Portsmouth, NH: Heinemann.

Driver, R. (1983). *The pupil as scientist?* Buckingham, England: Open University Press.

Driver, R., Guesne, E., & Tiberghien, A. (Eds.). (1985). *Children's ideas in science.* Buckingham, England: Open University Press.

Drummond, M. J. (1994). *Learning to see: Assessment through observation.* York, ME: Stenhouse.

Educational Testing Service. (1995). *Focus 28: Capturing the power of classroom assessment.* Princeton, NJ: Educational Testing Service.

Exploratorium Institute for Inquiry. (1998). *Professional development tools for inquiry-based science, ice balloons: Exploring the role of questioning in inquiry.* San Francisco: Author. Available on the World Wide Web at http://www.exploratorium.edu/ifi/activities/iceballoons/iceballoons.html

Gallas, K. (1995). *Talking their way into science: Hearing children's questions and theories, responding with curricula.* New York: Teachers College Press.

Hein, G. E., & Price, S. (1994). *Active assessment for active science: A guide for elementary school teachers.* Portsmouth, NH: Heinemann.

Loucks-Horsley, S., Carlson, M. O., Kapitan, R., Kuerbis, P. J., Clark, R. C., Melle, G. M., Sachse, T. P., & Walton, E. (1990). *Elementary school science for the 90's: A guide to action.* Andover, MA: The National Center for Improving Science Education, The NETWORK Inc., and Alexandria, VA: Association for Supervision and Curriculum Development (ASCD).

Love, N. (2002). *Using data/getting results: A practical guide for school improvement in mathematics and science.* Norwood, MA: Christopher-Gordon.

National Research Council. (1999). *Inquiry and the national science education standards: A guide for teaching and learning.* Washington, DC: National Academy Press.

Osborne, R., & Freyberg, P. (1985). *Learning in science: The implications of children's science.* Auckland, New Zealand: Heinemann.

Raizen, S. A., Baron, J. B., Champagne, A. B., Haertel, E., Mullis, I. V., & Oakes, J. (1989). *Assessment in elementary school science education.* Andover, MA: National Center for Improving Science Education, The NETWORK Inc.

Saul, W., & Reardon, J. (Eds.). (1996). *Beyond the science kit: Inquiry in action.* Portsmouth, NH: Heinemann.

Shapiro, B. L. (1994). *What children bring to light: A constructivist perspective on children's learning in science.* New York: Teachers College Press.

WestEd. (2001). Spreading the word on continuous assessment. *R&D Alert, 3*(3), 9. San Francisco: WestEd.

Index

**CORWIN
PRESS**

The Corwin Press logo—a raven striding across an open book—represents the happy union of courage and learning. We are a professional-level publisher of books and journals for K-12 educators, and we are committed to creating and providing resources that embody these qualities. Corwin's motto is "Success for All Learners."